NO GAME PLAN,
NO
VICTORY.
www.GamePlanForLife.com
Sam's CLUB
TOYOTA

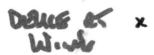

WRITERS:
Barry Cram, Brian Gass

**PROJECT LEADER,
ART DIRECTOR & DESIGNER:**
Darin Clark

CONTENT EDITOR:
Brian Gass

PRODUCTION EDITOR:
Juliana Duncan

CONTRIBUTORS:
Brian Daniel, Dale McCleskey,
Stacey Owens

VIDEO PRODUCER:
Justin Diel

VIDEO DIRECTOR:
William H. Cox

VIDEO EDITOR:
Tim Cox

**DIRECTOR, LEADERSHIP AND
ADULT PUBLISHING**
Bret Robbe

**MANAGING DIRECTOR, LEADERSHIP
AND ADULT PUBLISHING**
Ron Keck

Published by LifeWay Press®
©2010 Joe Gibbs

ISBN: 978-1-4158-6837-9
Item 005259409

Dewey decimal classification: 248.842
Subject Heading: CHRISTIAN LIFE \ MEN \ YOUNG MEN

Scripture quotations marked HCSB® are taken from the Holman Christian Standard Bible®, Copyright 1999, 2000, 2002, 2003 by Holman Bible Publishers. Used by permission. Scripture taken from the New American Standard Bible, Copyright © 1960, 1962, 1963, 1968, 1971, 1972, 1973, 1975, 1977, 1995 by the Lockman Foundation. Used by permission. (www.lockman.org)

Photos used by permission from Joe Gibbs Racing, NASCAR Media Group, and I Am Second.

To order additional copies of this resource, write LifeWay Christian Resources Customer Service; One LifeWay Plaza; Nashville, TN 37234-0113; fax order to (615) 251-5933; call toll-free (800) 458-2772; order online at *www.lifeway.com*; e-mail *orderentry@lifeway.com*; or visit the LifeWay Christian Store serving you.

Printed in the United States of America

Leadership and Adult Publishing
LifeWay Church Resources
One LifeWay Plaza
Nashville, TN 37234-0175

SPECIAL THANKS TO JOE GIBBS RACING
Dave Alpern, Phyllis Blair, Bob Dyer, Joe and Pat Gibbs, Barry Leventhal, Cindy Mangum, Don Meredith, Chuck Merritt, Jenni Murphy, David Wagner

Contents

How to Use This Study

TEAM TRAINING

Team Training refers to the group experience that takes place during your weekly meeting. It includes the video teaching as well as the Bible study portion. A summary of each part of the group experience follows.

PREGAME

Each weekly session begins with a Pregame warm-up that includes prayer, an encouraging word from the Team Captain, and a brief review of the previous week's Personal Training. Every group member has a chance to participate from the start.

KICKOFF

The session continues with a video object lesson from the Joe Gibbs Racing (JGR) shop, followed by an icebreaker question or two that again give every member a chance to participate in the study and to connect with one another.

FIRST HALF

The bulk of the video teaching occurs during the first half, with Joe illustrating the topic with experiences from his own life and an "assistant coach" or expert sharing more in-depth teaching on the topic in an interview format. Group members are encouraged to take notes that can be discussed later during Halftime and throughout the group Bible study in the Second Half.

HALFTIME

Halftime provides the men an opportunity to debrief the video and interact with a question about the weekly topic.

SECOND HALF

The small group Bible study occurs in the Second Half and focuses upon passages from the Bible with which the video is connected. Questions are experiential and guide members on a journey toward personal growth and spiritual transformation.

2-MINUTE WARNING

The 2-minute Warning is a time to wrap up the study by summarizing the main points and to encourage application in the coming week. The group also spends time in prayer at the end of the 2-minute Warning.

PERSONAL TRAINING

Personal Training is done individually as a follow-up to the group experience. Members may choose to study this deeper look into the topic throughout the week or in one sitting. During alternate weeks, there is an additional contemporary article that illustrates the topic for the week.

DAILY WORKOUTS

These reflections are for those members who would like a guide from *Game Plan for Life* as they do their daily quiet time or devotions with God. Members are encouraged to share from these experiences the following week.

Additional devotion materials are available at Joe's Web site which can be accessed through www.LifeWay.com/GamePlan or directly at www.GamePlanForLife.com.

BONUS MATERIALS

Many additional resources can be found throughout each week's session including suggested reading, movie ideas, Internet resources, and links to free video presentations.

www.LifeWay.com/GamePlan is your home for anything related to the Game Plan for Life family of products. Links are included to sites referenced throughout the study to help the Team Captain and group members find supplemental resources.

To keep up with the latest news and events related to Game Plan for Life and the Gibbs team, you may also go to **www.GamePlanForLife.com**.

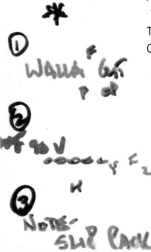

Joe Gibbs

A successful organization starts with its people

This has long been the philosophy o
Joe Gibbs. It helped carry him to three Supe
Bowl championships and the Pro Football Hal
of Fame as head coach of the NFL's Washingtor
Redskins, and has been a defining principle
behind building Joe Gibbs Racing (JGR) into
one of NASCAR's most successful multi-team
racing organizations.

It also guides Gibbs' latest project
Game Plan for Life, which is the title of his
New York Times Best Selling book and its
corresponding ministry (www.gameplanforlife
com). Once again, Gibbs assembled an amazing
team of eleven experts to respond to the issues
a national survey revealed to be the mos
pressing in men's lives. The results are a moderr
day game plan for a successful life based or
God's Word.

JGR has experienced amazing success
and growth since Gibbs founded the operatior
in 1991. Beginning its first season of racing
in 1992 with just 18 crew members, JGR now
employs close to 450 people. Despite the
immense growth, the company remains
defined by the same principles of its founder
integrity, a relentless work ethic, determination
perseverance, and team building.

Those principles have been the driving
force behind JGR's success including over 160
overall wins in NASCAR, three NASCAR Cup
Series championships (2000, 2002, and 2005
and back-to-back NASCAR Nationwide Series
Championships (2008 Owner's Champions and
2009 Driver and Owner's Champions).

Gibbs was applying character-based leadership long before he started in NASCAR. After 17 years of serving as an assistant coach to several college and NFL teams, Gibbs was hired as head coach of the Washington Redskins in 1981 and his determination and perseverance was immediately on display when the team lost its first five games. The Redskins rebounded to finish that season 8-8 and the following season, he would lead the Redskins to their first Super Bowl Championship in franchise history. Over the decade that followed he would lead the Redskins to two more Super Bowls, including victories in Super Bowl XXII following the 1987 season and Super Bowl XXVI after the 1991 season.

Over that time he became one of the winningest coaches in NFL history, but he retired from the NFL following the 1992 season to turn his attention to his family and the new race operations. Four years later, in 1996, Gibbs received the NFL's highest honor with induction into the Pro Football Hall of Fame.

JGR made its debut in 1992, but it was a year later that JGR would claim its first victory, when Dale Jarrett won the 1993 Daytona 500, known as the Super Bowl of racing, in the No. 18 Interstate Batteries car.

From that first victory the growth and success of JGR has been extraordinary. In 1999 Gibbs realized that multi-car teams were becoming more prevalent and successful than their single-car counterparts. He brought Tony Stewart into the Cup Series with crew chief Greg Zipadelli and sponsor The Home Depot.

The collaboration was successful from the outset. Bursting onto the NASCAR Cup scene in the No. 20 Home Depot car, Stewart became the winningest rookie in series history, with three wins en route to the Rookie of the Year title and a fourth-place position in the championship point standings.

In 2000, the No. 18 team with Bobby Labonte and the No. 20 team with Stewart proved to be a formidable one-two punch. The two drivers combined to win 10 of the series' 34 races, with Labonte winning four events en route to his first career NASCAR Cup Series championship. Just two years later it was Stewart's turn, as the Indiana native scored three wins during the 2002 campaign and captured his first NASCAR title.

In 2004, Gibbs shocked the sports world when he accepted an opportunity to return to the NFL for the team and fans he loved. With his eldest son J. D. running the day-to-day operations at JGR, Gibbs would be joined at the Washington Redskins by his youngest son Coy, who served as an offensive assistant on his coaching staff. Once again Gibbs went to work and in 2005 the franchise returned to the playoffs and earned its first playoff victory in six years.

While Gibbs was working to restore the Redskins winning tradition, the team he built at JGR continued to flourish. In 2005, JGR expanded to a third team as FedEx came on board to sponsor the new No. 11 team. That same year Stewart captured his second and JGR's third Cup Series Championship. Denny Hamlin joined the No. 11 FedEx team and went on to earn 2006 NASCAR Rookie of the Year honors.

One of the greatest challenges of Gibbs' career would come in his final season with the Redskins in 2007 when star player Sean Taylor was murdered in his Miami home. Despite the tragedy, Gibbs managed to steer the Redskins to victories in their final four games to secure yet another playoff season for the team.

When the season concluded, Gibbs made the decision to spend more time with his family and is now back with son J. D. at JGR. Coy left his post at the Redskins following the 2006 season to start JGRMX, a professional motocross team based near JGR's NASCAR operations in Huntersville, NC. Just as JGR had done in NASCAR, in just the first race of only its second season, JGRMX captured its first victory in January 2009 when rookie rider Josh Grant won in the season opener in Anaheim, CA.

When Gibbs returned to JGR prior to the start of the 2008 season, he had a new manufacturer, Toyota, a new sponsor for the No. 18 team, M&Ms, and a new driver, Kyle Busch. In addition, JGR learned during the season that Tony Stewart would be leaving after the conclusion of the racing season to start his own race team. But despite all the changes, JGR proved its foundation strong once again as Busch won a remarkable eight times in the Cup Series and, for the first time, all three JGR drivers qualified for NASCAR's Chase for the Cup.

2009 saw the debut of Joey Logano, a talented driver who became the youngest ever to start the Daytona 500 at the age of just 18 when he climbed behind the wheel of the No. 20 Home Depot Toyota. Further, he became the youngest winner in NASCAR history when he captured his first win at New Hampshire in June. Surrounding Logano is a support system that includes not only his veteran crew chief, Greg Zipadelli, but a foundation of nearly 450 JGR employees that was built over the past 19 years. The results speak volumes as Logano became the youngest ever to earn NASCAR Rookie of the Year honors. Hamlin also won a career-high four times and earned an impressive fifth-place finish in the standings, while Busch added yet another four victories.

In addition to his working daily with J. D. at JGR and Coy at JGRMX, as well as working to further spread the message of *Game Plan for Life*, Gibbs remains committed to Youth For Tomorrow, a home he founded in Bristow, VA that is now licensed to house up to 106 troubled boys and girls ages 11-18. He also added another championship to his resume when he coached his grandson Jackson's eight-man JEFA football team to a title this past fall.

Gibbs and his wife Pat currently reside near JGR's Huntersville, NC, headquarters and enjoy spending time with their eight grandchildren.

YOU
ARE BEING
SCOUTED

PREGAME

 Open with prayer.

Goals:

....

....

....

....

....

Kickoff

 TEAM CAPTAIN // PLAY VIDEO:
"Session 01 – You Are Being Scouted" ·······▶

 ◀-------

 Take a moment to think back to when you were in college or high school. Describe your favorite teacher or coach who made a difference in your life.

FiRST HALF

 TEAM CAPTAIN // RESUME VIDEO ·····························▶

Use the space provided below to take notes or jot down
key thoughts that come from this video segment.

....

....

....

....

....

....

....

....

....

....

Halftime

 In the video, Ken and Joe talked about how the concept of the Trinity
is the foundation for why God is a relational God.

What do you think about the idea that God wants to have a
relationship with you?

Second Half

 Background of key stories:

- ✖ Israel was one of several nations that fell under the mighty arm of the Midianites.
- ✖ The Midianites did not occupy Israelite territory, but they would invade them on a seasonal basis—at harvest time.
- ✖ They Midianites (and their allies) would actually camp out in huge numbers and then raid the crops (see Judges 7:12).
- ✖ The strength and tactics of the Midianites forced the Israelites to hide themselves and their harvest. This is why we find Gideon hiding while working.

Read Judges 6:11-24 out loud. Afterwards, answer the questions:

Judges 6:11-24

¹¹ *The Angel of the Lord came, and He sat under the oak that was in Ophrah, which belonged to Joash, the Abiezrite. His son Gideon was threshing wheat in the wine vat in order to hide it from the Midianites.* ¹² *Then the Angel of the Lord appeared to him and said: "The Lord is with you, mighty warrior."*

¹³ *Gideon said to Him, "Please Sir, if the Lord is with us, why has all this happened? And where are all His wonders that our fathers told us about? They said, 'Hasn't the Lord brought us out of Egypt?' But now the Lord has abandoned us and handed us over to Midian."*

¹⁴ *The Lord turned to him and said, "Go in the strength you have and deliver Israel from the power of Midian. Am I not sending you?"*

¹⁵ *He said to Him, "Please, Lord, how can I deliver Israel? Look, my family is the weakest in Manasseh, and I am the youngest in my father's house."*

¹⁶ *"But I will be with you," the Lord said to him. "You will strike Midian down as if it were one man."*

¹⁷ *Then he said to Him, "If I have found favor in Your sight, give me a sign that You are speaking with me.* ¹⁸ *Please do not leave this place until I return to You. Let me bring my gift and set it before You."*

And He said, "I will stay until you return."

¹⁹ *So Gideon went and prepared a young goat and unleavened bread from a half bushel of flour. He placed the meat in a basket and the broth in a pot. He brought them out and offered them to Him under the oak.*

20 *The Angel of God said to him, "Take the meat with the unleavened bread, put it on this stone, and pour the broth on it." And he did so.*

21 *The Angel of the LORD extended the tip of the staff that was in His hand and touched the meat and the unleavened bread. Fire came up from the rock and consumed the meat and the unleavened bread. Then the Angel of the LORD vanished from his sight.*

22 *When Gideon realized that He was the Angel of the LORD, he said, "Oh no, Lord GOD! I have seen the Angel of the LORD face to face!"*

23 *But the LORD said to him, "Peace to you. Don't be afraid, for you will not die."* 24 *So Gideon built an altar to the LORD there and called it Yahweh Shalom. It is in Ophrah of the Abiezrites until today.*

1 Describe God's feelings, attitudes, and actions toward Gideon throughout this entire exchange.

2 How did Gideon initially respond to God?

3 Is Gideon's second response (v. 15) to God more along the lines of humble, realistic self-assessment or faithless deprecation?

4 What captured your heart/attention the most—God's attitude or Gideon's response? Why?

5 Threshing wheat in a winepress shows Gideon's fear as well as his small harvest. But God approached Gideon like a head football coach recruiting a star player. Why?

6 In the video, Joe talked about the four ways God has proven Himself as personally real. When do you think God became more real or engaging to Gideon? What are some ways God has revealed Himself to you as passionate and engaged?

[COACH'S KEY POINT] WE ALL HAVE A PERSONAL VIEW OF GOD. HOWEVER, THERE IS ONLY ONE CORRECT WAY TO KNOW AND UNDERSTAND HIM—THROUGH JESUS.

Read aloud these two passages from the Bible and answer the following questions:

"*Man does not see what the* LORD *sees, for man sees what is visible, but the* LORD *sees the heart*" (1 Samuel 16:7).

"*For the eyes of the* LORD *range throughout the earth to show Himself strong for those whose hearts are completely His*" (2 Chronicles 16:9).

7 In what ways has God noticed you and brought His strength to bear in your life?

8 Both of these verses reveal something about how God looks at us. How does God look at things differently than we do?

9 If you were to fully embrace the notion that God considers you a first-round draft pick, how would it change the way you relate to God?

[COACH'S KEY POINT] WE EACH NEED TO ACCEPT GOD'S LOVE IN ORDER TO LIVE A TRULY SUCCESSFUL AND RELEVANT LIFE.

"'For I know the plans I have for you'—this is the Lord's declaration—'plans for your welfare, not for disaster, to give you a future and a hope'" (Jeremiah 29:11).

God truly does have a game plan for your life.

2-minute warning

Main takeaways:

✗ Just as the crew chief is the head of the race team, God is our crew chief or head coach for life. He oversees the big picture and cares deeply about each of us personally and the details of our lives.

✗ No matter how unknowable and big you think God is, He wants to have a relationship with you.

✗ God is searching throughout all the earth to recruit any and all who will decide to follow Him.

✗ God cares about and strengthens those who are committed to Him.

From our point of view, Gideon was a less-than-ideal candidate to lead an army for God. Yet God was scouting him like a first-round draft pick. He saw something in Gideon that we probably never would have seen. God looked past who Gideon was and saw what he could be—what he was created to be!

PRAYER REQUESTS

....

....

....

....

....

....

WHO IS GOD?

Almost everything we do is impacted by our view of God. Our values, beliefs, and even our everyday home lives are based on our view of God. So how do we formulate our concept of Him? What are the things that impact our personal view of Him? In a recent article entitled, "Americans Are Exploring New Ways of Experiencing God," the Barna Group revealed that 71% of Americans say they are more likely to develop religious beliefs on their own, and not necessarily to accept an entire set of beliefs that a particular church teaches. [1]

In the same article, about an equal amount of people felt that God was motivating them to stay connected to Him—but in different ways than they had done so in the past.

To a certain degree, it is good to accept the truth about God based on our experiences. But our view of God cannot be developed based on our experiences alone. According to *USA Today*, a little more than 90% of people say they believe in God, but they have four distinct views of His personality and engagement in human affairs. The researchers dubbed these categories as Authoritarian, Benevolent, Critical, and Distant.[2]

We all experience the same God but can interpret Him in different ways. It makes sense considering we are all different. We can interpret (or misinterpret) who God is based on who we are, what we have done, and what we

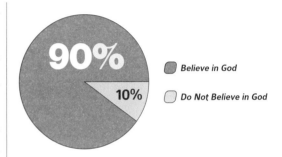

have experienced—good or bad. That's why we need more than experience. We need to settle on the truth about who He is. God is a Trinity (three in one) of Father, Son, and Holy Spirit. It is through the Trinity that we best relate to God and experience His love for us.

So the question still remains—how has God revealed Himself?

What we see in the sky tells us there is a God.

"The heavens declare the glory of God, and the sky proclaims the work of His hands" (Psalm 19:1).

Become a fan of Game Plan for Life on Facebook // www.facebook.com/GamePlanForLife

What we see on the earth tells us there is a God.

"From the creation of the world His invisible attributes, that is, His eternal power and divine nature, have been clearly seen, being understood through what He has made" (Romans 1:20).

What we know in our hearts to be true because of our conscience tells us there is a God.

"They [Gentiles] show that the work of the law is written on their hearts. Their consciences testify in support of this" (Romans 2:15).

Not only has God revealed Himself in these ways, but He has also revealed how He relates to us through the work of the Trinity—the Father, Son, and Holy Spirit.

Let's look at few verses that show how the Trinity is working together toward the same end. This collection of Scriptures describes how the "Holy Huddle" is planning and executing the Greatest Play of all time. The teamwork here is incredible.

First, God the Father is revealed as Love, and He sent the Son for us:

[16] *"For God loved the world in this way: He gave His One and Only Son, so that everyone who believes in Him will not perish but have eternal life.* [17] *"For God did not send His Son into the world that He might judge the world, but that the world might be saved through Him"* (John 3:16-17).

Second, Scripture teaches us that Jesus is revealed as the Light:

ATTRIBUTES OF GOD

ATTRIBUTES	DESCRIPTION	REFERENCE
Eternal	He is not bound by time.	Psalm 90:2
Immutable	He is unchanging and unchangeable—He can be trusted.	James 1:17
Omnipresent	He is everywhere.	Psalm 139:7-12
Omniscient	He knows all actual and possible things.	Psalm 147: 4-5
Omnipotent	He is all-powerful.	Revelation 19:6
Just	He is fair in moral judgments.	Acts 17:31
True	He is in agreement and is consistent within the Trinity.	John 14:6
Free	He is independent from all His creatures.	Isaiah 40:13-14
Holy	He is separate and free from all sin.	1 John 1:5
Sovereign	He is Supreme Ruler over everything at all times.	Ephesians 1:3-14

"Then Jesus spoke to them again: 'I am the light of the world. Anyone who follows Me will never walk in the darkness but will have the light of life'" (John 8:12). Also, Jesus sent the Holy Spirit:

The Holy Spirit was sent to counsel us on all things Jesus.

Finally, the Son receives the glory from the Holy Spirit—only to pass it back to God the Father:

I am the light of the world. Anyone who follows Me will never walk in the darkness but will have the light of life.

– Jesus Christ

[25] *"I have spoken these things to you while I remain with you.* [26] *But the Counselor, the Holy Spirit—the Father will send Him in My name—will teach you all things and remind you of everything I have told you"* (John 14:25-26).

See also John 15:26:

"When the Counselor comes, the One I will send to you from the Father—the Spirit of truth who proceeds from the Father—He will testify about Me."

Third, the Scripture records that the Spirit was sent to be our Leader in this life. He leads us to glorify the Son:

[13] *"When the Spirit of truth comes, He will guide you into all the truth. For He will not speak on His own, but He will speak whatever He hears. He will also declare to you what is to come.* [14] *He will glorify Me [Jesus], because He will take from what is Mine and declare it to you"* (John 16:13-14).

"Jesus spoke these things, looked up to heaven, and said: 'Father, the hour has come. Glorify Your Son so that the Son may glorify You'" (John 17:1).

So, God sends the Son. The Son sends the Holy Spirit (who is also sent by God). The Holy Spirit then makes much of the Son. And the Son makes much of God. This play is even better than the "triple-

Find Out for Yourself

1) Google **"Antony Flew"** to find out who he is and why he changed his mind about God.

2) Check Wikipedia for background on the **Intelligent Design** debate.

option, flea-flicker, Statue of Liberty" play to win the Super Bowl! It is better because this is, was, and always will be God's plan to win our hearts back to Him. This plan glorifies a holy God, and at the same time offers us a relationship with Him. Each member of the Trinity works the plan to glorify God and to bring us back to Him.

Here's the bottom line: we have an opportunity to have a relationship with God because of what He has done for us. But we need to come to Him on His terms. As you read the Scriptures and God reveals Himself to you more and more, SEE IT for what it is—truth. Jesus said that those seeking to worship God must worship Him in spirit and truth (see John 4:24).

The next thing you must do is to ACT ON IT. James wrote that Abraham believed and obeyed God. Because of this, he was found to be a righteous friend of God (see James 2:23).

The last thing you need to do is just LIVE IT. If you have come this far, continue to walk by faith, trusting that knowing and having a relationship with God—the Creator of our hearts and souls—is the only thing that will ultimately satisfy your heart. Paul expressed it like this:

> [7] "But everything that was a gain to me, I have considered to be a loss because of Christ. [8] More than that, I also consider everything to be a loss in view of the surpassing value of knowing Christ Jesus my Lord" (Philippians 3:7-8). ◪

1. "Americans Are Exploring New Ways of Experiencing God," *Barna Group* [online], 8 June 2009 [cited 5 April 2010]. Available from the Internet: www.barna.org.
2. "View of God Can Predict Values, Politics," *USA Today* [online], 12 Nov. 2006 [cited 5 April 2010]. Available from the Internet: www.usatoday.com.

DAILY WORKOUTS

MONDAY

In Joe's book *Game Plan for Life*, Ken Boa sums up three different ways that three different famous men have responded to their understanding of God:

- One man knew there was more out there in life, but kept going to church—searching for more.

- Another man realized it would make sense to want to talk to God in a crisis situation—if he only believed in Him.

- The last man discovered that God really is love, and that He is pursuing us.

All these guys had smarts (as Joe would say), but they all came to different conclusions about God in their lives. Can you identify with any of these three men? Have you journeyed through one or all of these ideas?

NOTES

For more team info and resources visit // **www.LifeWay.com/GamePlan**

TUESDAY

"For God loved the world in this way: He gave His One and Only Son, so that everyone who believes in Him will not perish but have eternal life" (John 3:16).

Do you remember the first time you heard this verse from the Bible? What do the words reveal about God's heart for the world and for you? Replace "the world" with your name and let that truth settle in your heart today.

NOTES

WEDNESDAY

In the NFL or NASCAR, there are fundamentals that lay the foundation for each team member. Consider these verses fundamental for your life:

[38] *"For I am persuaded that neither death nor life, nor angels nor rulers, nor things present, nor things to come, nor powers,* [39] *nor height, nor depth, nor any other created thing will have the power to separate us from the love of God that is in Christ Jesus our Lord!"* (Romans 8:38-39).

Take a moment to respond to God for promising you that truth.

NOTES

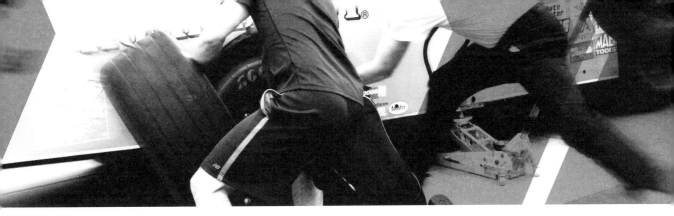

THURSDAY

In Joe's book *Game Plan for Life*, Ken Boa wrote about the role of the Holy Spirit in our lives. Jesus promised that after He left, He would send the Holy Spirit to come and be our Guide. Read John 14:1-31 and use the space below to list all the promises from Jesus about the Holy Spirit and His attributes.

NOTES

FRIDAY

"Knowing God and receiving His love are the most important things we can do. They are the keys to loving ourselves . . . and therefore being able to love our wives, children, and others. Our failure to live in the reality of God's love creates a restlessness that will show itself in all kinds of hurtful ways" (Ken Boa, *Game Plan for Life*).

Think about the ways in which your relationship with God has affected your relationships with those closest to you. Write down (and follow through with) any actions or attitudes you need to change to make those family relationships healthier.

NOTES

 *Check out Joe's video devotions at //* **www.LifeWay.com/GamePlan**

THIS COACH IS A TRUE HERO

Kris Hogan

DID YOU HEAR about the high school football game in 2008 played between Grapevine Faith Lions and Gainesville State School Tornadoes? Kris Hogan, the head coach of the Christian school's football team, turned the world of sports upside-down that night!

Grapevine Faith is a Christian school with many resources. Gainesville is a maximum-security facility that houses juveniles—some of whom have lost their families, freedom, and hope because of bad choices and crimes committed.

Here is what Coach Hogan asked the parents, fans, and cheerleaders to do for the other team:

1. Make a 40-yard spirit line though which the opposing team could run out onto the field.
2. Make a banner saying "Go Tornadoes!" for players to crash through at the end of the game.
3. Sit on the Gainesville side to cheer for players—all by name.
4. Send the cheerleaders over to the other side to cheer for the team.
5. Prepare for each player a goodie bag for the ride back home (which included a burger and fries, a soda, some candy, and a Bible with a letter from a Faith player).

It was a strange experience for boys whom most people cross the street to avoid. "We can tell people are a little afraid of us when we come to the games," says Gerald, a lineman who will wind up doing more than three years. "You can see it in their eyes. They're lookin' at us like we're criminals. But these people, they were yellin' for us! By our names!"

After the game, all the players met in the middle of the field. Isaiah, one of the Gainesville State players asked to pray. "Lord, I don't know how this happened, so I don't know how to say thank You, but I never would've known there was so many people in the world that cared about us."

"Here's the message I want you to send," Hogan wrote, "You are just as valuable as any other person on planet Earth."

Essentially, Coach Hogan asked his team to give the kids on the other team hope. And in doing so, Coach Hogan won the hearts of the players of the opposing team. Sounds a little like what God has done for us.[1]

Coach's Key Point

We are all made in God's image; therefore, we all have the need to be loved and to love others. Only after we have experienced God's love for us can we truly love others the way God wants us to.

1. Rick Reilly, "There are some games in which cheering for the other side feels better than winning.," *ESPN The Magazine* [online], 23 Dec. 2008 [cited 4 Apr. 2010]. Available from the Internet: http://sports.espn.go.com.

THE
ULTIMATE
PLAYBOOK

PREGAME

 Open with prayer.

Briefly discuss last week's *Personal Training.*

Kickoff

 TEAM CAPTAIN // PLAY VIDEO:
"Session 02 – The Ultimate Playbook"

 Describe a time when you felt as though your life was completely out of balance. What were the circumstances surrounding that experience? When did you finally realize your condition and what brought about that awareness?

First Half

▶ TEAM CAPTAIN // RESUME VIDEO ·······▶

Use the space provided below to take notes or jot down
key thoughts that come from this video segment.

....

....

....

....

....

....

....

....

....

....

Halftime

If you can, describe a time when you felt that the Bible had "come
alive" and was speaking directly to you.

What did God say through His Word? How did you respond?

Second Half

C Background of key stories:

- ✘ Jeremiah the prophet's ministry included the last 40 years of Judah's history—being called by God in the middle of King Josiah's reign. (Josiah was Judah's last good king.)
- ✘ Jehoiakim, Josiah's son, was a typical politician. He switched his allegiance from Egypt to Babylon when Babylon was victorious, and then back to Egypt when Egypt was victorious.
- ✘ King Jehoiakim was not a good king in God's eyes—unlike his father.
- ✘ This account takes place in the middle of winter where it can get very cold in Jerusalem.
- ✘ King Jehoiakim was probably in his winter apartment where a firepot was kept for heating purposes.

Read aloud the Bible passages and answer the following questions as a group. Pay close attention to the actions of Jeremiah and King Jehoiakim as you consider your personal views of the Bible as well.

Jeremiah 36:1-3

¹ **In the fourth year of Jehoiakim son of Josiah, king of Judah, this word came to Jeremiah from the LORD:**

² **"Take a scroll, and write on it all the words I have spoken to you concerning Israel, Judah, and all the nations from the time I first spoke to you during Josiah's reign until today. ³ Perhaps, when the house of Judah hears about all the disaster I am planning to bring on them, each one of them will turn from his evil way. Then I will forgive their wrongdoing and sin."**

1 Why do you think it is important that God had Jeremiah write His words down rather than just speaking them?

2 What seems to be the reason God delivered this message to Jeremiah? What was God's desire?

3 In the video, Joe gave an example of the Bible's relevance in his life. How have you and your family personally benefitted from God's written Word?

[COACH'S KEY POINT] THE BIBLE IS MORE THAN A BOOK; IT IS A SPECIFIC MESSAGE TO US FROM GOD.

Jeremiah 36:20-24

20 *Then they came to the king at the courtyard, having deposited the scroll in the chamber of Elishama the scribe, and reported everything in the hearing of the king.* 21 *The king sent Jehudi to get the scroll, and he took it from the chamber of Elishama the scribe. Jehudi then read it in the hearing of the king and all the officials who were standing by the king.* 22 *Since it was the ninth month, the king was sitting in his winter quarters with a fire burning in front of him.* 23 *As soon as Jehudi would read three or four columns, Jehoiakim would cut the scroll with a scribe's knife and throw the columns into the blazing fire until the entire scroll was consumed by the fire in the brazier.* 24 *As they heard all these words, the king and all of his servants did not became terrified or tear their garments.*

4 Jehoiakim's act of literally cutting out the very words of God communicates a rebellious heart. In what areas of your life have you figuratively done the same thing?

5 How are Jehoiakim's actions similar to Josh McDowell's approach to God's Word initially? What do you think caused their responses to be so different?

"For I assure you: Until heaven and earth pass away, not the smallest letter or one stroke of a letter will pass from the law until all things are accomplished" (Matthew 5:18).

"Heaven and earth will pass away, but My words will never pass away" (Matthew 24:35).

6 How do Jesus' words in Matthew 5:18 and 24:35 relate to the story in Jeremiah 36? If the Bible really is God's playbook for life, to what degree are Jesus' words comforting to you? Why?

[COACH'S KEY POINT] JESUS WAS AND IS WHO HE CLAIMED TO BE—GOD. HE WAS ALSO A MAN.

"For the word of God is living and effective and sharper than any two-edged sword, penetrating as far as to divide soul, spirit, joints, and marrow; it is a judge of the ideas and thoughts of the heart" (Hebrews 4:12).

7 Hebrews 4:12 reveals the nature of God's Word—that it is alive and active in us and through us. Share about a time recently when God's Word penetrated your soul.

God's heart about His own Word is revealed in this frequently-cited passage from the Old Testament:

4 *"Listen, Israel: The L*ORD *our God, the L*ORD *is One.* 5 *Love the L*ORD *your God with all your heart, with all your soul, and with all your strength.* 6 *These words that I am giving you today are to be in your heart.* 7 *Repeat them to your children. Talk about them when you sit in your house and when you walk along the road, when you lie down and when you get up.* 8 *Bind them as a sign on your hand and let them be a symbol on your forehead.* 9 *Write them on the doorposts of your house and on your gates"* (Deuteronomy 6:4-9).

8 After reading that passage, think about the quarterback on the field who receives the play from the coach, but then looks at his wrist to see the play and remember it. What practical things can you do to constantly keep God's Word in front of you?

16 *"All Scripture is inspired by God and is profitable for teaching, for rebuking, for correcting, for training in righteousness,* 17 *so that the man of God may be complete, equipped for every good work"* (2 Timothy 3:16-17).

[COACH'S KEY POINT] YES, THE BIBLE TALKS ABOUT MEN AND WOMEN AND THEIR PURPOSE, BUT I'VE ALSO LEARNED THAT WHEN YOU ARE A BELIEVER, IT HAS AN UNUSUAL ABILITY TO SPEAK DIRECTLY TO YOU.

2-minute warning

 Main takeaways:

- ✗ Just as the surface plate is perfectly level and serves as a constant reference for the race car, the Bible is our guide for life.

- ✗ God's Word is reliable and true. It will stand the test of time and eternity.

- ✗ The Bible is alive and active, and can reveal the deep and truest things about you.

- ✗ God's desire is that you study and saturate your mind with His Word so that you can live it out.

Think about the miracle of God's Word given to mankind. The Bible is 66 different books, written and preserved over 4,000 years, compiled and translated into hundreds of languages, revealing the truth about God's heart and love for you. The Bible records God's intervention for us and the relationship He has desired for so long with all of humanity. This book truly is God's ultimate playbook for life. And you can read it, study it, examine it, and enjoy it right now!

PRAYER REQUESTS

....

....

....

....

....

....

....

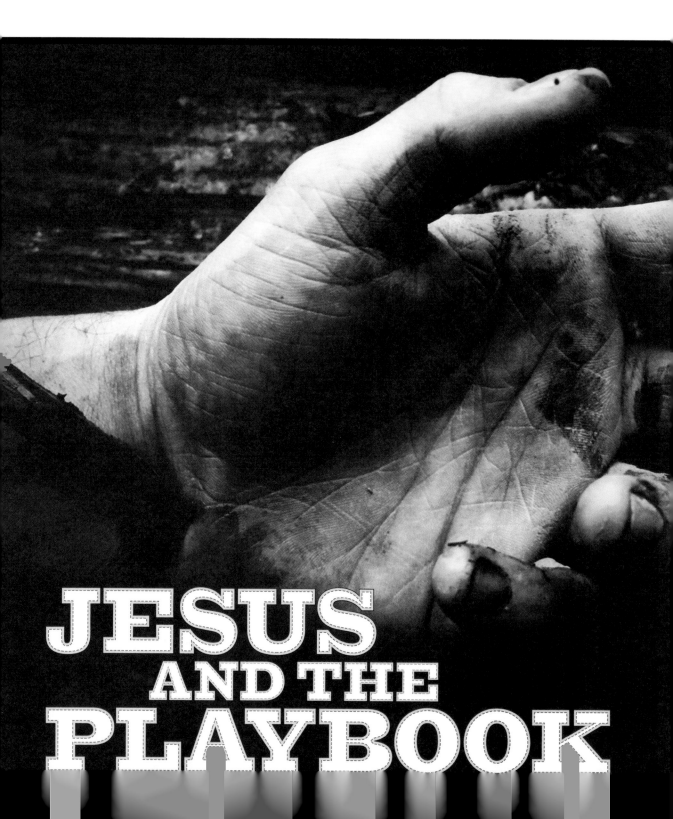

JESUS AND THE PLAYBOOK

Did you know that Jesus and the Father had a conversation about the playbook before Jesus was sent into the world? From the sidelines of heaven above, the Coach sent His Son Jesus Christ onto the field to help us out. But just before Jesus came, the most amazing conversation happened between Jesus and God. They had a conversation about what was going to transpire—Jesus entering this world as a man. In this conversation between Father and Son, we see Jesus' attitude toward God's playbook:

⁵ *"Therefore, as [Jesus] was coming into the world, He said: 'You did not want sacrifice and offering, but You prepared a body for Me.* ⁶ *You did not delight in whole burnt offerings and sin offerings.'* ⁷ *Then I said, 'See, I have come—it is written about Me in the volume of the scroll—to do Your will, O God!'"* *(Hebrews 10:5-7).*

Throughout the Book of Hebrews, the author argues the superiority of Jesus Christ to the angels, Moses, and the Old Testament priestly ministry and function. In chapter 10, the author is explaining that Jesus Christ is the ultimate sacrifice for forgiveness of sin. The coming of Jesus would complete God's game plan to bring us back to Him.

Jesus *wanted* to follow the playbook.

This passage from the playbook reveals Jesus' attitude toward the Bible.

Notice that this conversation between God and Jesus centers on what God desires and does not desire. It also hinges upon what has already been written in the Bible about Jesus. Remember, up until this time, the Trinity has experienced uninterrupted community from eternity past. But now is the time for Jesus to leave heaven and become a man. It has been written in "the scroll" (referring to the prophecy in Psalm 40:6-8) that the second Person of the Trinity would come for one express purpose—to be the perfect sacrifice for sin.

Jesus understood this completely and accepted it. He understood the play call and did not argue with it. This play would be much more difficult than a vulnerable wide receiver running a crossing route across the middle of the field. Jesus would give His very life. He submitted to the will of God and

THE PROPHECY	THE FULFILLMENT	THE TIME SPAN
Born of a Virgin Isaiah 7:14	Luke 1:26-38	700 years
Born in Bethlehem Micah 5:2	Matthew 2:1; Luke 2:4-7	700 years
The time of His appearance Daniel 9:24-27	Luke 19:44; Galatians 4:4	538 years
Abandoned by His disciples Zechariah 13:7	Matthew 26:31; Mark 14:50	520 years
Pierced in His side Zechariah 12:10	John 19:34,37	520 years
His resurrection and exaltation Psalm 16:10 Isaiah 52:13; 53:10-12	Acts 2:25-32	1,000 years (Psalms) 700 years (Isaiah)
His ascension into heaven Psalm 68:18	Acts 1:9; Ephesians 4:8	1,000 years
A forerunner prepares His way Isaiah 40:3-5; Malachi 3:1	Matthew 3:1-3; Luke 3:3-6	700 years (Isaiah) 450 years (Malachi)

the words in the playbook. As a result, victory awaits all those who believe in Jesus Christ. The Scripture continues,

> [12] *"But this man, after offering one sacrifice for sins forever, sat down at the right hand of God.* [13] *He is now waiting until His enemies are made His footstool.* [14] *For by one offering He has perfected forever those who are sanctified"* (Hebrews 10:12-14).

Find Out for Yourself

HISTORICITY OF THE BIBLE

Google "**Biblical Archeological Discoveries**" and find out why the field of archeology overwhelmingly supports the historicity of the Bible.

This passage in Hebrews is not the only place in Scripture where prophecy is mentioned or fulfilled. The Old Testament contains hundreds of prophecies regarding the coming Messiah, all of which were fulfilled in the Person of Jesus Christ. But this passage in Hebrews clearly reveals Jesus' love for and desire to follow God's Word.

Jesus *needed* to follow the playbook.

But that was not the only time Jesus referred to God's Word. As a man walking the earth, Jesus found Himself needing God's Word to execute this ultimate play perfectly. Once, Jesus was led into the wilderness where the Enemy confronted Him with a great defense. It was an all-out blitz—to tempt the very Son of God to sin and disobey the Father. With each temptation, Jesus responded with the only strategy He knew would work. When Satan tempted Jesus to break His fast, He responded:

"It is written: Man must not live on bread alone" (Luke 4:4).

When Jesus was tempted to break fellowship with the Father and worship the Enemy, Jesus answered him,

"It is written: Worship the Lord your God, and serve Him only" (Luke 4:8).

The third time, the Enemy twisted the Scriptures and tried to use them against Jesus. So when Jesus was tempted to prove He was the Son of God by His own power and wisdom, Jesus answered him,

12 "'It is said: Do not test the Lord your God.' 13 After the Devil had finished every temptation, he departed from Him for a time" (Luke 4:12-13).

Because Jesus knew He needed to rely on God's Word, He was willing to memorize it and use it as a defense against the Enemy. Having Scripture in His mind kept Him strong in the face of temptation and allowed Him to keep His relationship with God perfect (see Psalm 119:9-16). This was all a part of the preparation for executing the ultimate play.

Jesus *had* to follow the playbook.

Throughout the course of Jesus' ministry, the Gospels show Jesus quoting the Old Testament about 200 times from 24 different books.

Even though Jesus remained faithful to God and ultimately won the battle over the Enemy, it did not mean He would always feel like He was going to be victorious. Just before Jesus was to be betrayed by Judas (and then face the crucifixion on the cross), He was overwhelmed with emotion.

Coach's Key Point

The God of the Bible changes the lives of individuals who take His words to heart.

36 "Then Jesus came with them to a place called Gethsemane, and He told the disciples, 'Sit here while I go over there and pray.' 37 Taking along Peter and the two sons of Zebedee, He began to be sorrowful and deeply distressed. Then He said to them, 38 'My soul is swallowed up

Jesus on the Big Screen

LUTHER

Watch the movie *Luther* (2003) starring Joseph Fiennes with your family or friends. After it's over, talk about the common day opposition to God's Word that you experience today. Discuss how far you would go to stand up for God and His Word.

in sorrow—to the point of death. Remain here and stay awake with Me'. ³⁹ *Going a little farther, He fell facedown and prayed, 'My Father! If it is possible, let this cup pass from Me. Yet not as I will, but as You will'"* (Matthew 26:36-39).

In His moment of greatest need, Jesus prayed to God for help, and expressed His first and original attitude toward God's will and Word that was reflected before He came into this world. When it was all said and done, Jesus' attitude (the bottom line of His heart) never changed. He had to follow God's playbook no matter how great the cost. "Not My will, but Yours, be done" (Luke 22:42) was the battle cry from the very beginning to the very end.

Surely you have watched one of those sports shows or DVDs that chronicle the all-time greatest plays in sports history. Think about the best play you have ever seen on the field. To what degree do you think those great plays on the field actually resemble the plays that were drawn up in the playbook? They were probably drawn up one way, but executed with some variance.

God's ultimate play for saving mankind and for saving you was drawn up perfectly, executed perfectly, and fulfilled the perfect plan.

We know how Jesus approached the Scriptures, but what about you? How do you approach the Bible? Do you approach it with a Monday-morning quarterback, Lay-Z-Boy®, with-a-coozie-in-your-hand attitude? If so, you may always be second-guessing God. You could be uncertain about what God really wants for your life.

Then again, you may approach the Bible more like the passionate, face-painted, dedicated season ticket holder who would never miss a game if his life depended upon it.

Better still, you may love the playbook because you are on God's team; you're a team player doing the best you can to get it right. This is what God desires. If you study His Word, applying it as instructions for your life, you will be equipped to fulfill your purpose in life, helping others along the way. ◾

VIDEO REVIEW

Watch extra footage of Joe's interview with Josh McDowell at **www.LifeWay.com/GamePlan.**

SEE SESSION 2 VIDEO LINK ON THE WEB SITE.

GO DEEP

RECOMMENDED RESOURCES FOR DEEPER EXPLORATION ABOUT THE BIBLE

>> ***New Evidence That Demands a Verdict*** by Josh McDowell

>> ***The Case for Christ*** by Lee Strobel

>> ***The Reason for God*** by Timothy Keller

DAILY WORKOUTS

MONDAY

There are 176 verses in Psalm 119. Pick any ten verses in that chapter. Read them aloud to yourself and write down the one that stands out the most (choose carefully—you will be using this verse all week). What does God think about His Word? What needs to change in your own heart to value God's Word more?

NOTES

TUESDAY

In Joe's book *Game Plan for Life*, Josh McDowell lists the six most common false assumptions about the Bible:

- The Bible is just another man-made book.
- The Bible is full of myths and legends.
- The Bible was written by people who had little firsthand knowledge of the actual events.
- The Bible was written and copied by hand, so it is full of mistakes.
- The Bible's reliability cannot be proven by outside sources.
- The Bible doesn't make any difference in how people live.

Which of these have you believed before or still struggle with today? In the space below, write down when it was in your life (and the circumstances surrounding) that you believed God's Word to be true. If you have never made that decision, read the verse you wrote down for Monday. By faith, choose to believe God's Word today.

NOTES

....

....

....

WEDNESDAY

When was the last time you needed a big, bright, flashlight to show you the way in the darkness? Psalm 119:105 says, "Your word is a lamp for my feet and a light on my path." Where do you need God's light and direction the most in your life? Ask God to show you His wisdom from His Word this week.

NOTES

....

....

....

THURSDAY

In *Game Plan for Life*, Josh McDowell describes a very rigorous protocol for the ancient scribes to copy the Scriptures. Here are just a few examples: "[1] not even the shortest word could be copied from memory; everything had to be copied letter by letter. [2] The scribes had to count the number of times each letter of the alphabet occurred in each book and make sure it matched exactly the count in the original. [3] If a copied manuscript was found to contain even one mistake, the whole manuscript was discarded."

Read the verse you wrote down for Monday, and pray that God would give you a renewed reverence and respect for His Word.

NOTES

_____

_____

_____

FRIDAY

¹ *"In the beginning was the Word, and the Word was with God, and the Word was God.* ² *He was with God in the beginning.* ³ *All things were created through Him, and apart from Him not one thing was created that has been created.* ⁴ *Life was in Him, and that life was the light of men...* ¹⁴ *The Word became flesh and took up residence among us"* (John 1:1-4, 14).

Today, center your mind's attention and heart's affection on Jesus Christ, the Living Word. He is as real as the Bible you are reading. He is the Word who fulfills God's Word for all eternity.

NOTES

_____

_____

SESSION 03

MAKING GOD'S TEAM

PREGAME

Open with prayer.

Briefly discuss last week's *Personal Training*.

KickOff

TEAM CAPTAIN // PLAY VIDEO:
"Session 03 – Making God's Team"

Take a moment to think about the carefree fun kids are supposed to experience. If you can, describe an experience or memory in your childhood when you felt as though you were just "coasting carefree."

FIRST HALF

▶ **TEAM CAPTAIN // RESUME VIDEO** ┈┈┈┈┈┈┈▶

Use the space provided below to take notes or jot down
key thoughts that come from this video segment.

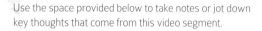

....
....
....
....
....
....
....
....
....
....

Halftime

In the video, Chuck Colson asserted that "playing on God's team" is a
very good analogy, and that we actually are "switching teams" when
we choose to accept Christ. How do you respond to that comment?

What does that imply about those who want to play on neither team?

Second Half

 Background of key stories:

- ✘ The rich ruler was considered part of the religious elite of the day—perhaps a member of the Sanhedrin or an official at the local synagogue.
- ✘ Zacchaeus would have probably been considered a social outcast because he worked for Rome as a tax collector.
- ✘ Just before these events, Luke chronicles a parable that involved a tax collector and a Pharisee (Luke 18:9-14).
- ✘ Asking about "inheriting eternal life" is the same as asking what it takes to enter the kingdom of God.
- ✘ We can assume the motives behind these men's actions were honorable. They truly wanted to know how to be right with God.

First read the story about Jesus and the rich man found in Luke 18:18-23. Then read the story between Jesus and Zacchaeus found in Luke 19:1-10. Afterwards, answer the questions.

Luke 18:18-23

¹⁸ *A ruler asked Him, "Good Teacher, what must I do to inherit eternal life?"*

¹⁹ *"Why do you call Me good?" Jesus asked him. "No one is good but One—God.*

²⁰ *You know the commandments: Do not commit adultery; do not murder; do not steal; do not bear false witness; honor your father and mother."*

²¹ *"I have kept all these from my youth," he said.*

²² *When Jesus heard this, He told him, "You still lack one thing: sell all that you have and distribute it to the poor, and you will have treasure in heaven. Then come, follow Me."*

²³ *After he heard this, he became extremely sad, because he was very rich.*

Luke 19:1-10

[1] *He entered Jericho and was passing through.* [2] *There was a man named Zacchaeus who was a chief tax collector, and he was rich.* [3] *He was trying to see who Jesus was, but he was not able because of the crowd, since he was a short man.* [4] *So running ahead, he climbed up a sycamore tree to see Jesus, since He was about to pass that way.*

[5] *When Jesus came to the place, He looked up and said to him, "Zacchaeus, hurry and come down, because today I must stay at your house."* [6] *So he quickly came down and welcomed Him joyfully.*

[7] *All who saw it began to complain, "He's gone to lodge with a sinful man!"*

[8] *But Zacchaeus stood there and said to the Lord, "Look, I'll give half of my possessions to the poor, Lord! And if I have extorted anything from anyone, I'll pay back four times as much!"*

[9] *"Today salvation has come to this house," Jesus told him, "because he too is a son of Abraham.* [10] *For the Son of Man has come to seek and to save the lost."*

1 Discuss for a moment the similarities between the experiences of the rich young ruler and Zacchaeus in Scripture. In what ways are they the same?

2 In what ways are their experiences different?

3 How did each man's attitude change during the course of his conversation with Jesus?

[COACH'S KEY POINT] JESUS WILL CHANGE YOUR LIFE.
HE WILL GIVE YOU SIGNIFICANCE AND RENEWED PURPOSE.

4. It seems the courage for Zacchaeus to make things right with other people came after his heart changed—after he joined God's team. Describe a similar experience in your own life once you decided to follow Christ, or the experience of someone you know if you have not yet made that decision.

Joe spoke of having the courage to follow Christ. With the courage of Zacchaeus in mind, read Matthew 16:24-26 and answer the following questions.

²⁴ *"If anyone wants to come with Me, he must deny himself, take up his cross, and follow Me.* ²⁵ *For whoever wants to save his life will lose it, but whoever loses his life because of Me will find it.* ²⁶ *What will it benefit a man if he gains the whole world yet loses his life? Or what will a man give in exchange for his life?"* (Matthew 16:24-26).

5. What does it mean to deny yourself and follow Christ? How is that related to playing on God's team? Describe the kind of courage it might take to live out this choice.

6. Why do you think the young, rich man went away sad? Was it a lack of courage, too much pride, etc.? What are some common obstacles that keep people from choosing God and from obeying His call?

[COACH'S KEY POINT] IN ORDER TO GET ON GOD'S TEAM, WE NEED TO ACCEPT CHRIST—ADMIT WE NEED HIM BECAUSE OF OUR SIN, AND ASK HIM TO COME AND LIVE IN US.

These next three passages cut straight to the heart of the choice between God's team and the Enemy's team. There is a definitive choice everyone must make. We can only play on God's team if we choose to trust in Christ.

[9] *"I am the door. If anyone enters by Me, he will be saved and will come in and go out and find pasture.* [10] *A thief comes only to steal and to kill and to destroy. I have come that they may have life and have it in abundance"* (John 10:9-10).

"I assure you: Anyone who hears My word and believes Him who sent Me has eternal life and will not come under judgment but has passed from death to life" (John 5:24).

"There is salvation in no one else, for there is no other name under heaven given to people, and we must be saved by it" (Acts 4:12).

[8] *"For you are saved by grace through faith, and this is not from yourselves; it is God's gift—* [9] *not from works, so that no one can boast"* (Ephesians 2:8-9).

7 There are only two teams for us to choose from—God's and Satan's. Have you made a decision to be on God's team? If you have never made that choice, would you want to make that decision now?

[COACH'S KEY POINT] GOD WILL FORGIVE YOU—NO MATTER WHAT YOU HAVE DONE.

8 Remember the beginning of this session? The Enemy wants us coasting carefree! But the apostle Paul once wrote, "When I was a child, I spoke like a child, I thought like a child, I reasoned like a child. When I became a man, I put aside childish things" (1 Corinthians 13:11). In which areas of your own spiritual life do you need to "put aside childish things" and follow God with serious intention, purpose, and thought?

2-minute warning

Main takeaways:

- ✗ Just as the stock car operates at an entirely different level than the soap box derby car, so do our lives once we have trusted in Christ. The Enemy wants you to coast downhill, but God wants you to live with His power to climb the hills in life.

- ✗ It takes courage to choose to follow Christ.

- ✗ No matter where you are on this spiritual scale, there is either a decision to make personally or a person to recruit for God's team.

Zacchaeus and the rich, young man had money and influence, yet they both came to Christ seeking more out of life. Jesus was willing to engage both of them without reservation. He did not—nor does He now—shun anyone who comes to Him with questions about God. Jesus' mission on this earth is pure and simple:

[16] *"For God loved the world in this way: He gave His One and Only Son, so that everyone who believes in Him will not perish but have eternal life.* [17] *For God did not send His Son into the world that He might condemn the world, but that the world might be saved through Him"* (John 3:16-17).

PRAYER REQUESTS

SESSION 03

BUILDING GOD'S TEAM

At the end of every football season, there is a constant presence of sports news and talk-show banter speculating about the future of "this head coach" and "that free agent." Who will lose their jobs? Who is guaranteed to stay? Who will get contract extensions? Which team will the star quarterback play for next? Each year, there are changes based on job performance of coaches and players. It all depends on upper management and whether or not they're interested in maintaining relationships with the players.

In this game of life with God as your Coach, there are no negotiations. There are no performance reviews that could get you kicked off the team. God never loses interest in you. When you've committed your life to Him, He is committed to you 100%. The promise is there:

> "for He Himself has said, I will never leave you or forsake you" (Hebrews 13:5).

Even though God promises to always be there for us, no one is forced to accept His offer. Consider the different ways you have responded to God over the years. Did you respond positively the first time you heard you could be on His team? Maybe it took a few times before it sank into your heart. People respond to God in different ways and for different reasons at different times in their lives.

Think about the professional football draft. Players are drafted in different rounds based on how good they are and how much the coach wants and needs them on the team. We learned in Session One that God seeks out everyone to play on His team. He is an "equal opportunity, no discrimination" coach who pursues us all. Yet not everyone who plays this game of life chooses to play on God's team. Why do you think some people choose not to join God's team? Let's look at various people who responded to Jesus in different ways.

When you think about all the people with whom Jesus or His followers had direct contact, there is a wide range of response. The religious elite of the day challenged Jesus' authority to supersede all the traditions they had set up over the years. To the degree that Jesus experienced pushback from religious people, He pushed back on them. At one point, Jesus replied:

7 "Hypocrites! Isaiah prophesied correctly about you when he said: 8 These people honor Me with their lips, but their heart is far from Me. 9 They worship Me in vain, teaching as doctrines the commands of men" (Matthew 15:7-9).

They rejected God and the message of Jesus because of their religion. They were doing many good things, but their hearts were in the wrong place.

When a religious man named Nicodemus wanted to speak with Jesus, he went to Him at night. Jesus spoke with Nicodemus and shared with him that "unless someone is born again, he cannot see the kingdom of God" (John 3:3). Nicodemus responded with confusion because he didn't fully understand what it meant to be "born again." Scripture does not record explicitly that Nicodemus became a Christian, but it

---

Jesus on the Big Screen

THE BLIND SIDE

Watch the movie *The Blind Side* (2009) with your family, friends, or small group. After it's over, discuss the importance of living an authentic Christian life, helping those who need it, and doing whatever it takes to obey God every day in every choice you make.

---

does say that he tried to defend Jesus in public (see John 7:49-51).

Nicodemus also helped prepare the body of Jesus for burial after the crucifixion. He brought very expensive spices and lotions (John 19:38-42). Perhaps he decided to join God's team in private, and then later made it public.

King Agrippa gives us another picture of one presented with the opportunity to join God's team:

27 "'King Agrippa, do you believe the prophets? I know you believe.'

28 Then Agrippa said to Paul, 'Are you going to persuade me to become a Christian so easily?'

29 'I wish before God,' replied Paul, 'that whether easily or with difficulty, not only you but all who listen to me today might become as I am'" (Acts 26:27-29).

The Bible gives us no proof that Agrippa chose to join God's team.

The reason there are so many different responses to Jesus is because there are so many conditions of the human heart. Jesus taught a parable and explained it this way:

3 "Then He told them many things in parables, saying: 'Consider the sower who went out to sow. 4 As he was sowing, some seeds fell along the path, and the birds came and ate them up. 5 Others fell on rocky ground, where there wasn't much soil, and they sprang up quickly since the soil wasn't deep. 6 But when the sun came up they were scorched, and since they had no root, they withered.

⁷ Others fell among thorns, and the thorns came up and choked them. ⁸ Still others fell on good ground, and produced a crop: some 100, some 60, and some 30 times what was sown. ⁹ Anyone who has ears should listen!" (Matthew 13:3-9).

After some time of confusion with His disciples about the teaching, Jesus later had to clarify the parable in plain words. (To read the entire exchange, see Matthew 13.) Jesus revealed four different situations that affect the way people respond to God's offer:

- Sometimes the activity of the Enemy snatches it away.
- Sometimes the shallow condition of the person's heart will not allow it to take deep root.
- Sometimes the worries of the world will choke it out.
- But sometimes the good and fertile condition of the heart will receive it, understand it, and bear fruit.

That is why we need to be aware of the people around us. The condition of their hearts is crucial in receiving the good news. We need to be ready to share the gospel message at a moment's notice.

To the men and women around you, you may be the only Christian equipped and ready to help them on their spiritual journey. There are so many unknowns to us that are known to God. We do not know who will cross our paths on a daily basis, but God does. We do not know the condition of their hearts, but God does. We do not know who is ready to switch teams and follow Christ, but God does. God is constantly looking for those who will help others find Him. This is what Jesus was trying to communicate during one of the last conversations He had with His followers after He was resurrected from the dead. His challenge is recorded in Matthew 28:19-20. Jesus said, "Go and make disciples, baptizing and teaching them!"

Coach's Key Point

Living life by any plan other than God's plan leaves us empty and asking, "Is this all there is in life?"

Think about it—you could introduce someone to God, and he or she could decide to play on His team! Take a look at the four statements listed below. If you committed these to memory, you could really help others see exactly what they need to do to know truth, receive fulfilling love, and get on God's team. These statements are not some sort of magical chant or special prayer in any way, but they contain essential truths that you should be excited to communicate to others so they know how to receive God's offer of salvation. Make it your goal to memorize these essential truths of Scripture:

- Our purpose is found in GOD. We were created by Him and for Him. He wants us to have a relationship with Him—to be on His team for life (see Colossians 1:16-17).
- Our problem is SIN. It separates us from God now (in this life) and in the future (eternity in hell). Our own game plan for life is not good enough (see Romans 3:23).
- Our solution is Christ's accomplished work on the CROSS. It was the ultimate game-winning play from His playbook. Jesus' death, burial, and resurrection conquered and defeated death and sin (see 1 Corinthians 15).
- We have only one action to take—BELIEVING. When we believe in Jesus' death and resurrection, we are declaring that we are switching teams and committing to play on God's team (see John 3:16; 5:24; Romans 3:20-24; Ephesians 2:8-9).

If someone asked you how to become a Christian, would you know what to say? Scripture says that once we have established Christ as Lord in our hearts, we should "always be ready to give a defense to anyone who asks you for a reason for the hope that is in you" (1 Peter 3:15). Be sensitive to those around you—family, friends, and coworkers. God wants to use you to reach others for His kingdom. Share with everyone you meet the good news God shared with you! ▣

Christ has liberated us to be free. Stand firm then and don't submit again to a yoke of slavery.

Galatians 5:1

VIDEO REVIEW

Watch extra footage of Joe's interview with Chuck Colson at **www.LifeWay.com/GamePlan**

SEE SESSION 3 VIDEO LINK ON THE WEB SITE.

GO DEEP

RECOMMENDED RESOURCES FOR DEEPER EXPLORATION ABOUT SALVATION

» *Born Again* by Charles W. Colson

» *Mere Christianity* by C. S. Lewis

» *The Sacred Romance* by John Eldredge

DAILY WORKOUTS

MONDAY

In the Bible, Jesus says:
"I am the way, the truth, and the life. No one comes to the Father except through Me"
(John 14:6).

The Bible also says:
"There is salvation in no one else, for there is no other name under heaven given to people, and we must be saved by it" (Acts 4:12).

Are these statements inclusive, exclusive, or both? Sometime today or this week, ask a couple of friends or coworkers to read these two verses, and then seek their opinion. If you get a chance, tell them about your own spiritual journey and why you are convinced of the importance of playing on God's team.

NOTES

_____

_____

_____

_____

_____

For more team info and resources visit // **www.LifeWay.com/GamePlan**

TUESDAY

"Instead, God has chosen what is foolish in the world to shame the wise, and God has chosen what is weak in the world to shame the strong" (1 Corinthians 1:27).

In Joe's book *Game Plan for Life,* Chuck Colson wrote about two big paradoxes that God taught him. He learned that "if you really want to find your life, you have to lose it for Christ's sake." Chuck also saw that "God didn't choose to use me when I was at the top. He used me when I was broken and at the bottom."

What is God trying to teach you about His design for your life? How do you think God wants to use you on His team?

NOTES

....

....

....

WEDNESDAY

[3] *"For I passed on to you as most important what I also received: that Christ died for our sins according to the Scriptures,* [4] *that He was buried, that He was raised on the third day according to the Scriptures,* [5] *and that He appeared to Cephas, then to the Twelve.* [6] *Then He appeared to over 500 brothers at one time"* (1 Corinthians 15:3-6).

Stop for a moment to think and meditate on the death, burial, and resurrection of Christ. What did that accomplish for you? How has that impacted your life? Share this with someone today.

NOTES

....

....

....

THURSDAY

In *Game Plan for Life*, Colson chronicled his journey from the White House to the big house where he spent time in prison for his crimes in the Watergate scandal. He recounted much of what he experienced in between. At one point, Colson stated, "I sat there a long time, deeply aware and ashamed of my own sin and desperate to know God. I didn't know the right words to pray. I simply called out to Him, asking Him to take me, to come into my life."

Do you know anyone who needs God, but may not know how to ask about Him? If you can, offer to help those around you take that first step toward God. You might consider sharing Chuck's story.

NOTES

FRIDAY

Coach says, "It's never too early to commit your life to Jesus Christ; and as long as you have breath, it's never too late, either." The apostle Paul once expressed his heart for his lost Jewish people in this way:

"Brothers, my heart's desire and prayer to God concerning them is for their salvation!" (Romans 10:1).

Take time to pray for the salvation of others you know who need God. Write their names down. Pray that their hearts would be open to respond to Christ.

NOTES

THIS TEAM
HAS TRUE GRIT

Have you ever heard of the "Iron Men" of Sewanee? In 1899 this college football team from a small, Episcopal university in Tennessee accomplished the unthinkable. They dominated college football in the South around the turn of the century.

Under the leadership of Coach Billy Sutter and captain "Diddy" Seibels, the Sewanee Tigers went undefeated:

- They went a perfect 12-0.
- They outscored their opponents 322 to 10.
- They defeated teams including Tennessee, LSU, Texas, and Texas A&M.
- Only one team, the University of Auburn, scored on the Tigers all year.
- Auburn was coached by John Heisman—the name's sake for the Heisman Trophy.
- The other eleven games were shutouts.[1]

As if that were not enough, here is where the "Iron Men" of Sewanee move from mere folklore to football legends. Between the six-day period from November 9th to 14th, they traveled 2,500 miles and played five away games. The "Iron Men" of Sewanee defeated five opponents in six days—with Sunday as their only day off! This is arguably the greatest road trip in college football history.

> "Winning five road games in six days, all by shutout scores, has to be one of the most staggering achievements in the history of the sport. If the Bowl Championship Series (BCS) had been in effect in 1899, there seems little doubt Sewanee would have played in the title game. And they wouldn't have been done in by any computer ratings."[2]
> —Joe Paterno, Penn State head coach

If you knew the outcome of a football season before it began, and you saw the "Iron Men" of Sewanee accomplish what they accomplished, would you still want to play for them? It takes courage to want to play for a team like that.

This experience sounds a lot like what God is offering us through His Son. God does not guarantee us riches or fame. He does not promise us an easy road or a comfortable lifestyle. God does not guarantee us that we will face an easy Opponent. But there is one thing God promises: we will play on the winning team.

Coach's Key Point

Jesus came into this world to save those who know they fall short of God's expectations. He came so we can become players on God's team.

1. "Can't Repeat: The 1899 Sewanee Iron Men," *Bleacher Report* [online], [cited 8 Apr. 2010]. Available from the Internet: http://bleacherreport.com.
2. "1899: A Sewanee Legend," *Sewanee* [online], [cited 8 Apr. 2010]. Available from the Internet: www2.sewanee.edu.

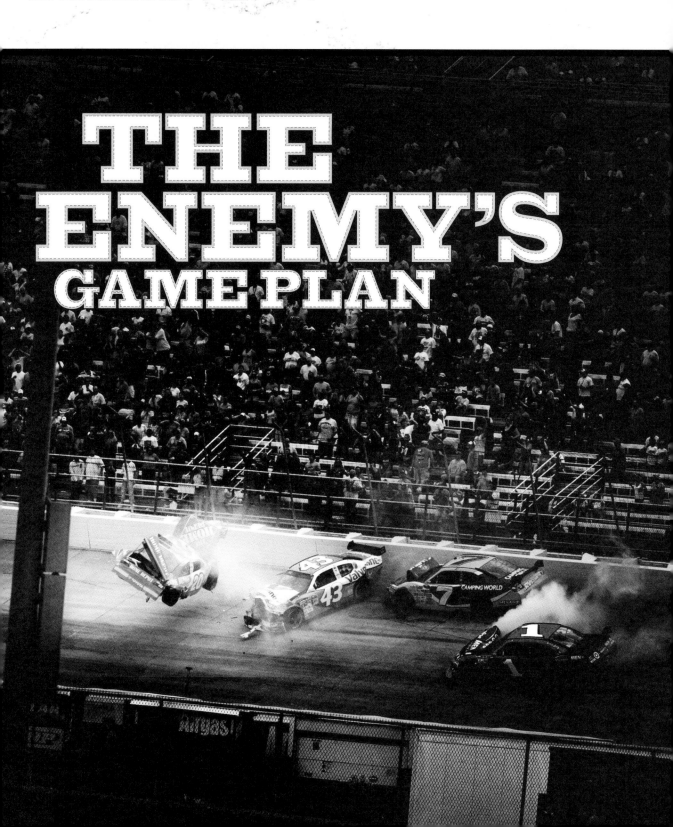

THE ENEMY'S GAME PLAN

PREGAME

 Open with prayer.

Briefly discuss last week's *Personal Training*.

Kickoff

 TEAM CAPTAIN // PLAY VIDEO:
"Session 04 – The Enemy's Game Plan"

 Think about the disappointment that comes with being disqualified. Was there ever a time growing up when this happened to you at an event? What feelings, thoughts, or words do you associate with being disqualified?

FirstHalf

 TEAM CAPTAIN // RESUME VIDEO ┄┄┄┄┄┄►

 Use the space provided below to take notes or jot down
key thoughts that come from this video segment.

Halftime

 How does this video reflect a change in the nature of the creation/
evolution conversation from just a generation ago?

What did you learn from the video that you had never heard before
in a science class?

Second Half

Background of key stories:

- ✖ Scripture is clear that the universe has a beginning. Science has discovered the same thing.
- ✖ Scripture is clear there is a progression in creation. Science has revealed the same thing.
- ✖ Scripture is clear that man was created last. Archaeology has revealed the same thing.
- ✖ Scripture is clear that mankind was created in God's image and in His presence. The Enemy would have you believe neither.

[COACH'S KEY POINT] SCIENCE AND THE BIBLE AGREE THAT THERE WAS A BEGINNING TO THE UNIVERSE [I.E., IT WAS CREATED]. THE UNIVERSE HAS NOT ALWAYS BEEN HERE.

In your Bible, read aloud Genesis 3:1-13, 22-24 and answer the following questions as a group.

Genesis 3:1-13, 22-24

¹ Now the serpent was the most cunning of all the wild animals that the LORD God had made. He said to the woman, "Did God really say, 'You can't eat from any tree in the garden'?"

² The woman said to the serpent, "We may eat the fruit from the trees in the garden. ³ But about the fruit of the tree in the middle of the garden, God said, 'You must not eat it or touch it, or you will die.'"

⁴ "No! You will not die," the serpent said to the woman. ⁵ "In fact, God knows that when you eat it your eyes will be opened and you will be like God, knowing good and evil." ⁶ Then the woman saw that the tree was good for food and delightful to look at, and that it was desirable for obtaining wisdom. So she took some of its fruit and ate it; she also gave some to her husband, who was with her, and he ate it. ⁷ Then the eyes of both of them were opened, and they knew they were naked; so they sewed fig leaves together and made loincloths for themselves.

⁸ Then the man and his wife heard the sound of the LORD God walking in the garden at the time of the evening breeze, and they hid themselves from the LORD God among the

trees of the garden. ⁹ So the Lᴏʀᴅ God called out to the man and said to him, "Where are you?"

¹⁰ And he said, "I heard You in the garden, and I was afraid because I was naked, so I hid."

¹¹ Then He asked, "Who told you that you were naked? Did you eat from the tree that I had commanded you not to eat from?"

¹² Then the man replied, "The woman You gave to be with me—she gave me some fruit from the tree, and I ate."

¹³ So the Lᴏʀᴅ God asked the woman, "What is this you have done?"

And the woman said, "It was the serpent. He deceived me, and I ate."

²² The Lᴏʀᴅ God said, "Since man has become like one of Us, knowing good and evil, he must not reach out, and also take from the tree of life, and eat, and live forever." ²³ So the Lᴏʀᴅ God sent him away from the garden of Eden to work the ground from which he was taken. ²⁴ He drove man out, and east of the garden of Eden He stationed cherubim with a flaming, whirling sword to guard the way to the tree of life.

1 What was the first and original lie the Enemy embedded into the heart of mankind? How has this lie changed over time?

2 To what degree has the distortion about the creation account affected you in your everyday life—home life, kids at school, conversations at work?

3 When the Enemy said, "God knows that when you eat it your eyes will be opened and you will be like God, knowing good and evil" (v. 5), he actually wasn't lying (see vv. 22-24). Yet, he said it as if it were a lie to challenge the goodness of God. How did Adam and Eve respond to the Enemy? In what ways did their innocence vanish before their eyes?

4 After Adam and Eve disobeyed, God still pursued them: "Where are you?" (v. 9). What do you think this says about the heart of God?

A couple of different times when Jesus was battling the religious elite of His day, He revealed some sinister facts about Satan and his game plan of deception:

[44] *"You are of your father the Devil, and you want to carry out your father's desires. He was a murderer from the beginning and has not stood in the truth, because there is no truth in him. When he tells a lie, he speaks from his own nature, because he is a liar and the father of liars.* [45] *Yet because I tell the truth, you do not believe Me"* (John 8:44-45).

"A thief comes only to steal and to kill and to destroy. I have come that they may have life and have it in abundance" (John 10:10).

5 Since the Enemy is the father of all lies, what are some ways the Enemy has lied to you—about God, others, or your purpose?

6 How have you responded to those lies? Which ones have you believed? Which one of those lies has caused the most damage in your life?

7 Describe the danger of doubting God's Word, both at the beginning of time and today. What are the implications and potential results?

8 In your own words, write down the specifics of the Enemy's game plan against you.

Read this passage, and think about the faith it takes to stop believing a lie:

⁵ *"Now if any of you lacks wisdom, he should ask God, who gives to all generously and without criticizing, and it will be given to him.* ⁶ *But let him ask in faith without doubting. For the doubter is like the surging sea, driven and tossed by the wind"* (James 1:5-6).

9 Asking God for wisdom requires what from you? In light of this imperative from James, name some practical ways you can battle the Enemy as you pursue the truth from God about all things.

[COACH'S KEY POINT] SCIENTISTS BELIEVE THERE IS ORDER TO THE UNIVERSE AND THAT IT CAN BE UNDERSTOOD BY HUMAN MINDS. THIS TAKES FAITH.

2-minute warning

⚙ Main takeaways:

✗ Just as NASCAR provides a template so each car can conform to the rules of the race, God has given us a template to follow in life. The Enemy wants to get us disqualified by distorting God's template.

✗ The Enemy will tell a lie, a half-truth, or the truth as if it were a lie in an effort to make you doubt God and His goodness.

✗ The Enemy is active to this very day—lying and distorting the truth about the beginning of our existence.

✗ God is the source of truth, and if you ask Him, He will give you wisdom to discern truth from lies.

At the end of his life, the apostle Paul declared, "I have fought the good fight, I have finished the race, I have kept the faith" (2 Timothy 4:7). There is a race for each one of us to run. At the end, there will be a standard that we are compared to. That standard is the image of Christ as a result of our having trusted in Him.

PRAYER REQUESTS

....

....

....

....

....

....

....

SESSION 04

CREATION
AND
SCIENCE

Throughout the centuries, the church in general has not always been on the right side of history, or science and discovery. Early in church history, because of a hyper-reaction to the Greek culture of the day, the church leadership refused to acknowledge that the earth was round. They said it was flat. This handful of intellectual church leaders rejected the influence of Greek culture—including the work geographers had done such as calculating the earth's circumference to within 50 miles.

With good intentions no doubt, the church was leery of the systems of the world. So, they rejected anything that couldn't be found specifically in Scripture.

Consider the great scientist, Galileo Galilei, born in 1564. He was a brilliant thinker—a mathematician, astronomer, and physicist. Many scientists today believe he is responsible for the birth of modern science. Yet there was a time when he faced opposition from the religious elite of his day. Galilei argued against the idea that the earth was the center of the universe. After the turn of the 17th century, he began to publicly teach that the sun was at the center of the universe. His ideas were met with bitter opposition. Galilei was actually denounced to the Roman Inquisition because of his theory.

Although he was personally cleared of any offense at the time, the Catholic Church condemned Galilei's beliefs as contradicting Scripture. Galilei was warned to abandon his conclusions about the universe. He did so for the sake of his life. But later he defended his views in his most famous work, *Dialogue Concerning the Two Chief World Systems*. He was tried by the Inquisition and found suspect of heresy. Galilei was forced to recant, spending the rest of his life under house arrest.

Fast-forward a few hundred years to the Scopes Monkey Trial in the early 1900s. Christians in progressive America thought it best to fight the Enemy's theory of evolution in the courts. At this point in history, the cultural divide between the traditionalists and the modernists had begun. In the little city of Dayton, Tennessee, in the summer of 1925, a jury was to decide the fate of John Scopes. He was a high school

Get the latest information on GPFL events and more. // *www.GamePlanForLife.com*

biology teacher who was charged with illegally teaching the theory of evolution. Tennessee's constitution prohibited that evolution be taught in public classrooms. The meaning of the trial transcended that small town; it symbolized the conflict between who would lead and shape the social, cultural, and intellectual landscape of the future.

These examples paint a spectrum for the Christ-follower to consider. What is the appropriate response to scientific discoveries? What role does God expect us to play in these discussions?

Well, did you know that Jesus specifically prayed for you concerning your involvement in this world? Before Jesus was crucified, He prayed for His disciples at the time and for those who would later believe:

> [11] "I am no longer in the world, but they are in the world, and I am coming to You. Holy Father, protect them by Your name that You have given Me, so that they may be one as We are one.

> [15] I am not praying that You take them out of the world but that You protect them from the evil one. [16] They are not of the world, as I am not of the world" (John 17:11,15-16).

Summary: Jesus prayed that God would not take His followers out of the world, but keep us in it. It's a peculiar situation—we are called to be in the world but not of the world. We are expected to be present enough in a worldly system to make God known to others by our lives, while at the same time keeping the world an arm's-length away so it doesn't influence our character.

What approach to science can you take? Begin by believing that God's Word is true in all matters of which it speaks, but acknowledge that it was not written as a technical science book. For example, the Scriptures record that "In the beginning God created the heavens and the earth" (Genesis 1:1). This is not a scientific observation, but it does involve all the elements scientists consider as they study: "In the beginning" denotes TIME; "God" explains the FORCE; "created" is MOTION; "the heavens" defines SPACE; and "the earth" consists of MATTER.

Since space, time, matter, motion, and force—all the elements of Einstein's theory of relativity—are contained in the

> *"All matter, energy, space, and time dimensions associated with the universe began at one fixed, predetermined, finite time. The 'Cause of the Universe' brings all the matter, energy, time, and space into existence."*

very first verse of the Bible, we should not be surprised that science and the Bible are, in fact, compatible.

Concerning Science

Although the Bible was not written as a science book, nothing discovered in the field of science will contradict what is found in the Bible. God's Word is scientifically accurate. If you believe the Bible, then you believe that the universe had a beginning. The Big Bang Theory was introduced in the early 1920s when scientists began to see that the universe is not constant and eternal. Scientists since the days of Aristotle wrongly believed that the universe had always existed. But Einstein's theory of relativity paved the way to think differently, and it has been proven over and over again. From the discovery of the Doppler effect to the more recent discovery of cosmic background radiation, science is unraveling the mysteries of God's creation at an astounding pace. But every layer harmonizes with Scripture and confirms what is written. No other religion in the world is as scientifically reliable.

Concerning History

Although the Bible was not written as just a history book, nothing discovered in the field of archeology will contradict the writings in the Bible. God's Word is historically accurate. Archeological digs in the biblical lands confirm Old Testament stories again and again. From the walls of Jericho falling outward away from the city, to the existence of the Hittites, to King Solomon's city gates and temple grounds, the historicity of the Bible is confirmed. Extra-biblical accounts of kings and empires, cities and towns,

Online Resources

Creation vs. Evolution is such a twentieth-century debate! It's obvious this universe has a beginning. The question is, how long ago was its beginning? Check out:

AnswersInGenesis.com (for those who believe in a young earth)

Reasons.org (for those who believe in an old earth)

Jesus on the Big Screen

EXPELLED

Watch *Expelled: No Intelligence Allowed* (2008). This documentary, hosted by Ben Stein, depicts intelligent design as an alternative to evolution, and claims it deserves a place in academia.

conquests and wars all confirm and corroborate the historical message and timeline of the Bible.

Concerning the Universe

Although the Bible was not written as an astronomy book, nothing discovered while searching the universe will contradict the writings in God's Word. What the Bible states about the universe is astronomically accurate. One theory to explain the universe is the theory of dark matter. Proving this theory would resolve many inconsistencies in current theoretical physics. Simply put, the theory suggests that there are particles in the universe, called dark matter, that we cannot see or measure, but that hold the universe together. First submitted by Fritz Zwicky, dark matter has been tagged "The God Particle." This might be more of an "average Joe" response to this theory, but Scripture says,

> [16] *"For everything was created by [Christ], in heaven and on earth, the visible and the invisible, whether thrones or dominions or rulers or authorities—all things have been created through Him and for Him. [17] He is before all things, and by Him all things hold together"* (Colossians 1:16-17).

Adapting this kind of approach with scientific discoveries will help you bridge the gap between the Bible and science in your own mind. What is not an option in our day and age is to disengage from the discussion—especially when the Enemy continues the assault on the existence of God and the beginning of the universe. Do not isolate yourself from all things worldly. If science discovers something new about the earth or the universe, study it through the lens of your faith in God. The issue is not whether you are right or wrong with regard to your scientific beliefs; the issue is being willing to engage in the conversation, while being open to the discoveries of science, then trusting God's Word always to be true. ◼

VIDEO REVIEW

Watch the full-length interview with John Lennox at **www.LifeWay.com/GamePlan**

SEE SESSION 4 VIDEO LINK ON THE WEB SITE.

GO DEEP

RECOMMENDED RESOURCES FOR DEEPER EXPLORATION ABOUT CREATION

>> *Darwin on Trial* by Phillip E. Johnson

>> *Why the Universe Is the Way It Is* by Hugh Ross

>> *The Privileged Planet (DVD)* by Illustra Media

DAILY

MONDAY

Let's begin at the beginning, and read Genesis 1. Count the times God says His creation is "good." Reflect on the fact that the "goodness of God" is revealed in His creation, and thank Him for being good to you.

NOTES

TUESDAY

In *Game Plan for Life*, John Lennox wrote a section entitled "We Do Not Have to Choose Between Science and God." What is your first response to that statement? In the past, how have you wrestled through the weighty matters of science and faith?

¹³ *"For it was You who created my inward parts; You knit me together in my mother's womb.* ¹⁴ *I will praise You, because I have been remarkably and wonderfully made. Your works are wonderful, and I know this very well"* (Psalm 139:13-14).

The same God who created this world created you. Meditate on the wonderful, greatness of God and who He is. Thank Him for being too big to figure out, and at the same time being accessible and interested in you.

NOTES

....

....

....

WEDNESDAY

*"The heavens are the L*ord's, *but the earth He has given to the human race"* (Psalm 115:16).

Over what parts of creation has God given you to be a good steward? Where in your life do you need to become a better steward of what God has created for you and given to you?

NOTES

....

....

....

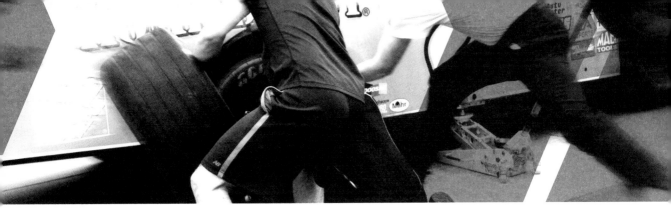

THURSDAY

While trying to explain why faith in God actually inspired the discipline of science, Lennox said, "the great pioneers of science, such as Galileo, Kepler, and Newton, expected to find law in nature because they believed in a Lawgiver."

These men believed in the same God who created and designed you for a purpose. When you think about God being active and interested in your life, what does that mean to you? What are you inspired to do in response?

NOTES

FRIDAY

[1] *"The heavens declare the glory of God, and the sky proclaims the work of His hands.* [2] *Day after day they pour out speech; night after night they communicate knowledge"* (Psalm 19:1-2).

Jesus once said that if we did not give praise to God that the rocks and "stones would cry out" (Luke 19:40). Do not let God's creation do all the talking today. Say a good word about God to someone who needs to hear it. Declare His glory in your own life.

NOTES

SIGNING BONUS

PREGAME

 Open with prayer.

Briefly discuss last week's *Personal Training.*

KickOff

 TEAM CAPTAIN // PLAY VIDEO:
"Session 05 – Signing Bonus"

 When was the last time you made an impulsive decision in life?
How equipped were you to handle the bumps that followed?
In hindsight, what do you wish you had known?

First Half

TEAM CAPTAIN // RESUME VIDEO ·············▶

Use the space provided below to take notes or jot down
key thoughts that come from this video segment.

....

....

....

....

....

....

....

....

....

Halftime

Have you ever experienced an "I-wish-I-knew-then-what-I-know-now"
moment in regard to your money?

Which of Ron's lessons have you since learned? Describe.

Second Half

Background of key stories:

- ✗ Jesus taught a lot about money in the New Testament.
- ✗ In this story, Jesus conveyed that money is an extension of a spiritual life.
- ✗ Jesus was speaking to the Pharisees—the religious elite of His day.
- ✗ The Pharisees were expecting the coming Messiah to establish a physical kingdom on earth.
- ✗ This could explain why Jesus compared "treasures on earth" to "treasures in heaven" in His teaching.
- ✗ Money (or *mammon* in some translations) is better understood as "wealth" or "property."

Read aloud Matthew 6:19-24 and answer the discussion questions as a group.

Matthew 6:19-24

[19] *Don't collect for yourselves treasures on earth, where moth and rust destroy and where thieves break in and steal.* [20] *But collect for yourselves treasures in heaven, where neither moth nor rust destroys, and where thieves don't break in and steal.* [21] *For where your treasure is, there your heart will be also.*

[22] *The eye is the lamp of the body. If your eye is good, your whole body will be full of light.* [23] *But if your eye is bad, your whole body will be full of darkness. So if the light within you is darkness—how deep is that darkness!*

[24] *No one can be a slave of two masters, since either he will hate one and love the other, or be devoted to one and despise the other. You cannot be slaves of God and of money.*

1 Why do you think Jesus' teaching about money was so definitive—so black and white?

2 When Jesus said, "The eye is the lamp of the body" (v. 22), He was communicating two things: (a) how you view material wealth will determine your spiritual health, and (b) the choice is yours to make. How do you view material wealth—with a healthy eye or a sick eye?

3 Take a moment to paint a picture of a man whose head coach in life is money. What actions, attitudes, relationships, and ambitions would likely develop and follow?

[COACH'S KEY POINT] WISE FINANCIAL DECISIONS HAVE THEIR FOUNDATION IN THE PRINCIPLES OF SCRIPTURE.

Paul expounded on Jesus' teaching about money and contentment with these words:

3 "If anyone teaches other doctrine and does not agree with the sound teaching of our Lord Jesus Christ and with the teaching that promotes godliness, 4 he is conceited, understanding nothing, but having a sick interest in disputes and arguments over words. From these come envy, quarreling, slander, evil suspicions, 5 and constant disagreement among men whose minds are depraved and deprived of the truth, who imagine that godliness is a way to material gain. 6 But godliness with contentment is a great gain.

7 For we brought nothing into the world, and we can take nothing out. 8 But if we have food and clothing, we will be content with these.

9 But those who want to be rich fall into temptation, a trap, and many foolish and harmful desires, which plunge people into ruin and destruction. 10 For the love of money is a root of all kinds of evil, and by craving it, some have wandered away from the faith and pierced themselves with many pains" (1 Timothy 6:3-10).

4 What do you think is the "great gain" that comes from "godliness with contentment" (v. 6)?

5 From this passage, describe the difference between making a lot of money and wanting to keep a lot of money.

6 People who want to be rich are setting themselves on a track that will "plunge people into ruin and destruction" (v. 9). What are some practical ways to avoid such spiritual ruin?

[COACH'S KEY POINT] FINANCIAL SUCCESS IS ACHIEVED WHEN
WE MANAGE WISELY THE MONEY GOD GIVES US TO FURTHER HIS
OBJECTIVES AND TRY TO ACCOMPLISH WHAT HE'S ASKED US TO
DO WITH IT.

One symptom of a heart that is not content is the inability to be generous with your money. Paul once bragged on the church he planted in the city of Corinth:

[6] *"Remember this: the person who sows sparingly will also reap sparingly, and the person who sows generously will also reap generously. [7] Each person should do as he has decided in his heart—not reluctantly or out of necessity, for God loves a cheerful giver. [8] And God is able to make every grace overflow to you, so that in every way, always having everything you need, you may excel in every good work"* (2 Corinthians 9:6-8).

7   What are some of the obstacles that have kept you from giving with a content, cheerful heart?

8   If your attitude is right when you give to God, what are the promises that God said would follow? How have you seen that in your life?

[COACH'S KEY POINT] REMEMBER: NET WORTH IS NOT A MEASURE
OF SELF-WORTH, AND NO AMOUNT OF MONEY IS EVER ENOUGH IN
ITSELF TO PROVIDE CONTENTMENT.

2-minute warning

Main takeaways:

✗ Just as the seven-post shaker helps the team master the changing conditions on a race track, God's principles for finances help us master our money.

✗ How you handle your money is a reflection of your relationship with God.

✗ Learning contentment is the key to applying God's principles for money management. This heart change will get you on the right track.

✗ God loves it when you give out of the goodness of your heart—without coercion or guilt.

In today's culture, it is tough to remain content with what you have. Paul found the secret of contentment when he centered his life on God. Jesus also warned us about becoming a slave of money so we need to heed that warning with all caution. You must master this in your life, men, or it will master you.

PRAYER REQUESTS

SHOW ME THE MONEY

Not everyone can be the valuable, franchise quarterback who gets the multi-million dollar signing bonus to play NFL football. Players like that are few and far between. Did you know that a quarterback recently took home the NFL's largest single-season paycheck ever? It was almost $28 million. Two of the top NFL quarterbacks are currently negotiating new contracts and if those negotiations go as expected, they each stand to make close to $20 million per season with a front-end signing bonus of $50 million.

Over the remainder of their careers, that could result in almost $200 million worth of paychecks. That's not too shabby.

This signing bonus is a good illustration of how God works in His economy. Here's the key to understanding it all: everyone gets a signing bonus! Let's take this to the next level: everyone gets the same signing bonus! Now, if you're looking at your paycheck compared to someone else's paycheck, you're missing the point. The bonus is not the material wealth we gain on this earth. The bonus is the eternal instructions found in the playbook. This is the signing bonus to which everyone has access. You just have to read it, study it, and apply it.

Everyone is born unique and different—your family situation, talents, interests, education, personal drive, life strategies, decisions—all of these play a role in how much money you will make. You may have wealthy parents that have given you a head start in life. You may have a work ethic that will not be compromised by slothfulness. You may have a knack for seeing and seizing early investment opportunities. Or maybe you have lost more money than you have made, but you keep getting up after you hit rock bottom and find a way to financially succeed again. There are many practical factors that determine where you will financially land in life.

When God drafted you to be on His team, you could be sure there was a signing bonus. God is not afraid to talk about wealth and money. As a matter of biblical fact, there are at least 800 different verses in the Scripture that speak to this subject. But the specific direction of those verses does not reveal how much God is going to bless you.

Get the latest information on GPFL events and more. // *www.GamePlanForLife.com*

THE ONLY 5 SHORT-TERM USES OF MONEY

5 BUCKETS TO BE FILLED

INCOME

GIVING TAXES INVEST/SAVE DEBT LIVING EXPENSES

These verses speak to how you should manage what God has given you. We will look at a few of them in the paragraphs below. You will discover that you should not judge how blessed you are based on the material wealth you acquire on this earth. This is the wrong standard. Instead, consider whether you glorify God with the money He's given you.

In the Bible study section of this lesson, you learned that there are sins associated with being wealthy. That does not mean it is wrong to want to make a lot of money. It just means it is wrong if you want to hoard a lot of money—always buying bigger houses, bigger cars, more stuff. Look at some of the financial guidelines God has left for us:

Bonus Tip #1 // **Proverbs 6:1-11** – If you do not work hard, you will probably be poor.

Bonus Tip #2 // **Proverbs 22:7** – When you borrow money to purchase something you cannot afford, you are choosing to enslave yourself to the lender.

Bonus Tip #3 // **Psalm 62:10** – Riches are not guaranteed in life, but you control the attitude of your heart.

Bonus Tip #4 // **2 Corinthians 9:7** – Being generous does not depend on how much you have.

Bonus Tip #5 // **2 Corinthians 9:7** – God is pleased when you learn to give generously—without compulsion or coercion.

Christian Giving

Notice that the more you read what God says about finances, the more you see that your wealth is meant to be a blessing to others—your family, friends, and those in need within your sphere of influence.

Find Out for Yourself

Money is mentioned over 800 times in the Bible. Use either an online concordance or Google **"money in the Bible"** to link to some of the references. Choose one to memorize or meditate upon each day this week.

WHAT MONEY IS NOT

MONEY IS NOT A MEASURE OF OUR SELF-WORTH.
See Ephesians 2:10; Deuteronomy 8:16-18.

MONEY IS NOT A REWARD FOR GODLY LIVING.
See 1 Corinthians 3:13-15; Hebrews 11.

MONEY IS NOT A GUARANTEE OF CONTENTMENT.
See Ecclesiastes 5:10; Philippians 4:11-13.

MONEY SHOULD NEVER DEFINE US.
See Jeremiah 9:23-24.

By reputation, Christ-followers are considered the most generous group in American society. In just the recent years approaching 2010, Barna Research has estimated 84 percent of adults (Christian, non-Christian, etc.) donated some money to churches or non-profit organizations—averaging just a few hundred dollars each. But the same research revealed that only 5 percent of adults tithed—that is, they gave one-tenth of their money to their church. Of that 5 percent who tithed, only 24 percent of them were evangelicals.

The reason Christians are known for their giving and generous spirit is because of Christ. He modeled the generous life on earth. He taught about giving and money as well. When studying New Testament principles of giving, always keep in mind what Jesus

"EVANGELICALS" ARE "BORN AGAIN" CHRISTIANS WHO:

1. say their faith is very important in their lives today;

2. believe they have a personal responsibility to share their religious beliefs about Christ with non-Christians;

3. believe that Satan exists;

4. believe that eternal salvation is possible only through grace, not works;

5. believe that Jesus Christ lived a sinless life on earth;

6. assert that the Bible is accurate in all that it teaches; and

7. describe God as the all-knowing, all-powerful, perfect deity who created the universe and still rules it today. Being classified as an evangelical is not dependent upon church attendance or the denominational affiliation of the church attended.[1]

Coach's Key Point

Seek God when making financial decisions. And do not be afraid to seek godly financial counsel.

DECISION MAKING

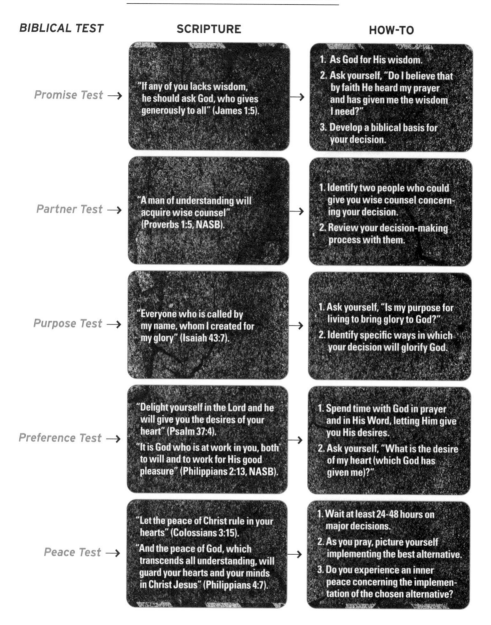

BIBLICAL TEST	SCRIPTURE	HOW-TO
Promise Test →	"If any of you lacks wisdom, he should ask God, who gives generously to all" (James 1:5).	1. As God for His wisdom. 2. Ask yourself, "Do I believe that by faith He heard my prayer and has given me the wisdom I need?" 3. Develop a biblical basis for your decision.
Partner Test →	"A man of understanding will acquire wise counsel" (Proverbs 1:5, NASB).	1. Identify two people who could give you wise counseling your decision. 2. Review your decision-making process with them.
Purpose Test →	"Everyone who is called by my name, whom I created for my glory" (Isaiah 43:7).	1. Ask yourself, "Is my purpose for living to bring glory to God?" 2. Identify specific ways in which your decision will glorify God.
Preference Test →	"Delight yourself in the Lord and he will give you the desires of your heart" (Psalm 37:4). "It is God who is at work in you, both to will and to work for His good pleasure" (Philippians 2:13, NASB).	1. Spend time with God in prayer and in His Word, letting Him give you His desires. 2. Ask yourself, "What is the desire of my heart (which God has given me)?"
Peace Test →	"Let the peace of Christ rule in your hearts" (Colossians 3:15). "And the peace of God, which transcends all understanding, will guard your hearts and your minds in Christ Jesus" (Philippians 4:7).	1. Wait at least 24-48 hours on major decisions. 2. As you pray, picture yourself implementing the best alternative. 3. Do you experience an inner peace concerning the implementation of the chosen alternative?

did concerning the Old Testament Law. Jesus never came to abolish anything from the Law. Instead, He came to fulfill it by establishing the New Covenant (Matthew 5:17).

Think of the Old Testament Law as a written code of conduct. When Jesus fulfilled the Old Testament Law, He showed that it was possible to keep the Law with a heart that is fully committed

MONTHLY BUDGET

ITEM	MONTHLY EXPENSE	PAYOFF AMOUNT
INCOME _____		
GIVING	_____	
SAVINGS	_____	
HOUSING		
1st Mortgage	_____	_____
2nd Mortgage	_____	_____
Maintenance	_____	
UTILITIES		
Electricity	_____	
Water	_____	
Gas	_____	
Phone	_____	
Cell	_____	
Trash	_____	
Cable	_____	
TRANSPORTATION		
1st Car Payment	_____	_____
2nd Car Payment	_____	_____
Gas/Oil	_____	
Maintenance	_____	
Car Insurance	_____	
FOOD	_____	
CLOTHING /HYGIENE	_____	
PERSONAL		
Health Insurance	_____	
Life Insurance	_____	
Child Care	_____	
Entertainment	_____	
Credit Cards	_____	_____
Other Payments	_____	
MISCELLANEOUS	_____	
TOTAL MONTHLY EXPENSES	_____	
SURPLUS/DEFICIT	_____	
(Income minus Expenses)	*Make sure this equals zero	

"But those who want to be rich fall into temptation, a trap, and many foolish and harmful desires, which plunge people into ruin and destruction."

– The apostle Paul, just before his death, writing to his young disciple Timothy (1 Timothy 6:9)

to the Father. With Jesus, it is not enough to just accomplish the duty of the Law by an act of will (letter of the law) if your heart is not right in the accomplishing of that Law (spirit of the law). Therefore, when Jesus fulfilled the Law, He shifted the focus off of the will to accomplish the letter of the law, and emphasized the attitude and motivation behind the action itself, which was what God always intended. God's desire was made clear by Moses:

"Listen, Israel: The Lord our God, the Lord is One. Love the Lord your God with all your heart, with all your soul, and with all your strength. These words that I am giving you today are to be in your heart" (Deuteronomy 6:4-6).

Jesus fulfilled the Law and demonstrated that life with God is a matter of obedience flowing from a heart committed to Him and empowered by His Holy Spirit.

When we look at Christian giving from that perspective, we begin to live in freedom rather than obligation. The issue is not whether you give or do not give; the issue has to do with whether your heart is right before God. If your heart is right, He will lead you to give cheerfully. This is at the very heart of grace. We are under no obligation to give a tithe as a requirement to be in good standing with God. Jesus has fulfilled the Law and we are under grace. This opens up a fulfilling life with God that is lived out of joy and a heart of gratitude. ✪

1. "New Study Shows Trends in Tithing and Donating," *Barna Group* [online], 14 Apr. 2008 [cited 6 Apr. 2010]. Available from the Internet: www.barna.org.

VIDEO REVIEW

Watch the full-length interview with Ron Blue at **www.LifeWay.com/GamePlan**

SEE SESSION 5 VIDEO <u>LINK</u> ON THE WEB SITE.

GO DEEP

RECOMMENDED RESOURCES FOR DEEPER EXPLORATION ABOUT FINANCES

>> *Faith-Based Family Finances* by Ron Blue and Jeremy White

>> *The Treasure Principle* by Randy Alcorn

>> *Your Money Counts* by Howard Dayton

DAILY WORKOUTS

MONDAY

Paul shared some great wisdom with Timothy to pass along to those in his church who had wealth:

[17] *"Instruct those who are rich in the present age not to be arrogant or to set their hope on the uncertainty of wealth, but on God, who richly provides us with all things to enjoy.* [18] *Instruct them to do what is good, to be rich in good works, to be generous, willing to share,* [19] *storing up for themselves a good reserve for the age to come, so that they may take hold of life that is real"* (1 Timothy 6:17-19).

Here are just a few questions to reflect upon as you consider this passage:

1. Where do you place your hope and confidence when it comes to wealth and provision? (v. 17)

2. Why do you want wealth in the first place? (v. 18)

3. What is "real" life? (v. 19)

Ask God to clarify this counsel in your heart and to help you develop goals and objectives that will honor Him with your earthly provision.

NOTES

....

....

....

....

....

TUESDAY

In Joe's book, *Game Plan for Life*, Ron says, "Contentment has nothing to do with money. True contentment comes when money and financial decisions do not dominate our thoughts." King Solomon said it like this:

"The one who loves money is never satisfied with money, and whoever loves wealth is never satisfied with income. This too is futile" (Ecclesiastes 5:10).

Take an inventory of the stuff in your life. Are there things keeping you from finding true contentment? What can you do without? Prayerfully consider what you need to do with all of your stuff.

NOTES

WEDNESDAY

In Luke 12:48, Jesus said:

"Much will be required of everyone who has been given much. And even more will be expected of the one who has been entrusted with more."

How do you initially respond to that statement? What has God given you, and what do you think He is going to require from you? Ask God to give you a vivid picture of what He wants you to do with what He has given you.

NOTES

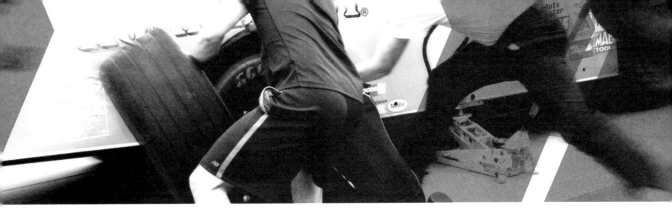

THURSDAY

In *Game Plan for Life*, Ron lists Four Principles of Financial Success:
1. Spending less than you earn
2. Minimizing your use of debt
3. Maintaining emergency savings
4. Thinking long-term

Rate yourself. How well do you utilize these four principles? With whom do you need to set an appointment and discuss your financial situation? Do not hesitate. Do it today!

NOTES

FRIDAY

⁹ *"Honor the* LORD *with your possessions and with the first produce of your entire harvest;* ¹⁰ *then your barns will be completely filled, and your vats will overflow with new wine"* (Proverbs 3:9-10).

Today is Friday, and chances are, it's also payday. Don't forget to honor God with your money. If you're not in the habit of giving to God, start this weekend. Begin the journey of generous living. Remember, you cannot outgive God.

NOTES

SESSION 06

PLAYING
HURT

PREGAME

Open with prayer.

Briefly discuss last week's *Personal Training.*

Kickoff

TEAM CAPTAIN // PLAY VIDEO:
"Session 06 – Playing Hurt" ·····················▶

When was the last time you really felt like you were part of a team?
What were the circumstances surrounding that experience? How did it
make an impact on your life?

First Half

▶ **TEAM CAPTAIN // RESUME VIDEO** ┈┈┈┈┈┈┈▶

Use the space provided below to take notes or jot down key thoughts that come from this video segment.

....

....

....

....

....

....

....

....

Halftime

Why is "learning to play hurt" a good analogy when talking about living life in this broken world—having to endure the damage of sin?

Do not share it now—you will get a chance in a few minutes—but just think for a moment about this question: if you could be free of one habitual sin (or nagging addiction), what would it be?

Second Half

 Background of key stories:

- ✖ The word "sin" is found about 100 times in the New Testament alone.
- ✖ In the Hebrew language, one word for "sin" means to deviate from the moral norm, to break or rebel against our relationship with God.
- ✖ In the Greek, another word for "sin" means to fall short or miss the mark (like coming up short when shooting at a target).
- ✖ The apostle Paul traces his own addictions and habitual failures back to sin.
- ✖ Paul always addresses the church as saints, not sinners, and once proclaimed that he was the "chief of sinners."

Read the following Scriptures aloud and then answer the discussion questions as a group.

James 1:13-15

[13] *No one undergoing a trial should say, "I am being tempted by God." For God is not tempted by evil, and He Himself doesn't tempt anyone.* [14] *But each person is tempted when he is drawn away and enticed by his own evil desires.* [15] *Then after desire has conceived, it gives birth to sin, and when sin is fully grown, it gives birth to death.*

Galatians 5:17

For the flesh desires what is against the Spirit, and the Spirit desires what is against the flesh; these are opposed to each other, so that you don't do what you want.

1 After reading those two passages, how would you define sin?

2 Why is sin so dangerous if left unchecked? How have you witnessed sin deal a deathblow to your life or to the lives of those around you?

3 God's law is perfect, yet sin takes advantage of the law and produces a desire in us to break it. In the video, when Ravi was describing why God gave us His law, he said "the rules are strict because the game is wonderful." How does this statement help you understand the goodness of God's moral law?

[COACH'S KEY POINT] GOD LOVES US AND IS INTERESTED IN OUR STRUGGLES. WITHOUT GOD, WE HAVE NOWHERE TO TURN FOR ANSWERS TO EXPLAIN THE EMPTINESS WE FEEL INSIDE. WITHOUT HIM, THERE'S NOWHERE TO TURN FOR HOPE.

Even though sin is very powerful, it can still be conquered because of what Jesus Christ accomplished on the cross. Paul makes this wonderful and definitive statement about our spiritual condition when he says:

[6] "For we know that our old self was crucified with Him in order that sin's dominion over the body may be abolished, so that we may no longer be enslaved to sin... [9] because we know that Christ, having been raised from the dead, will not die again. Death no longer rules over Him. [10] For in light of the fact that He died, He died to sin once for all; but in that He lives, He lives to God. [11] So, you too consider yourselves dead to sin, but alive to God in Christ Jesus.

[12] Therefore do not let sin reign in your mortal body, so that you obey its desires. [13] And do not offer any parts of it to sin as weapons for unrighteousness. But as those who are alive from the dead, offer yourselves to God, and all the parts of yourselves to God as weapons for righteousness. [14] For sin will not rule over you, because you are not under law but under grace" (Romans 6:6,9-14).

4. Remember the question we asked at Halftime—if you could be free of one habitual sin (or nagging addiction), what would it be? Discuss and encourage one another.

[COACH'S KEY POINT] WE MUST SEE OURSELVES AS WE REALLY ARE—AS SINNERS. WE HAVE ALL DELIBERATELY RUN FROM GOD AND REJECTED HIM. OUR SIN IS THE ROOT OF OUR SUFFERING AND STRUGGLES.

5 In the video, Ravi spoke about praying, reading the Bible, and accountability. To help you in your walk, which one of these do you need most? Why do you think this is important in your life right now?

[COACH'S KEY POINT] THE MESSAGE OF THE BIBLE IS THAT GOD OFFERS FORGIVENESS FOR SIN AND FREEDOM FROM THE HABITS AND ADDICTIONS THAT HOLD US. JESUS DIED ON THE CROSS TO RESTORE OUR BROKEN RELATIONSHIP WITH GOD.

The Scripture says that we should "encourage each other daily, while it is still called today, so that none of you is hardened by sin's deception" (Hebrews 3:13). It also says to "confess your sins to one another and pray for one another, so that you may be healed. The urgent request of a righteous person is very powerful in its effect" (James 5:16).

6 If you can, describe a time when you practiced this on a consistent basis. How did it help you cope with the sin and struggles in your life?

7 What common fears or obstacles do you think keep men from engaging in this kind of teamwork?

8 Like Ravi said in the video, encouragement and accountability are key if you want to overcome sin and addiction. If you are not meeting in a small group, to what degree would you be willing to continue meeting with a group of men for encouragement and accountability?

2-minute warning

 Main takeaways:

- ✗ Just as the pit crew is a support team keeping the race car running at optimal performance, we need men around us for encouragement, accountability, and support.

- ✗ Sin has affected every one of us. It is destructive and will cripple us in life.

- ✗ We need each other's encouragement in the game of life—God designed life to be a team sport!

- ✗ The responsibility is yours! You need to decide who gets to shape your life.

We each have a personal life story with plenty of drama, baggage, hurts, and wounds to go along with it. As much as others have hurt us, we have hurt others through our sin and neglect. The best thing you can do though, men, is to talk through your story, get help whenever you need it, and walk alongside other men who can help you stay in the game.

"Iron sharpens iron, and one man sharpens another" (Proverbs 27:17).

TEAM CAPTAIN // PLAY VIDEO:
"Joe's Closing Challenge"

PRAYER REQUESTS

....

....

....

....

....

....

....

FINISH STRONG

For the true competitor, there is nothing more satisfying than being able to say, "I gave it my everything. I laid it all out on the field, and I've got nothing left." Even if you lost the game and the sting of defeat is still reverberating in your heart, there is a certain satisfaction in knowing you played your heart out.

A great story from the world of sports came in 1994 when the New York Giants were playing the Dallas Cowboys in the NFC East championship game. Emmitt Smith embodied what it means to "play hurt."

"'I'm fine,' he lied to teammates, coaches, and trainers. 'Get out,' he told the backup who tried replacing him." Even though Smith had suffered a first-degree separation in his right shoulder, he pressed on, scoring the Cowboys' only touchdown of the game.

Smith refused to sit out because of his injury, but he did make one request

done. There is no sin big enough or bad enough to separate you from the Head Coach. "Who can separate us from the love of Christ? Can affliction or anguish or persecution?" (Romans 8:35). Answers: No one. No.

There are no wounds nor any addiction powerful enough to sideline you for the rest of your life. Refuse to

"I've heard about guys playing hurt. I wanted to play hurt and be effective."

of his offensive line: "Run behind me so you can pick me up."[1]

Finish Strong Because God Expects It

God expects you to play hurt because He knows that you can finish strong. The Bible is full of men who messed up pretty bad, but then walked with God to finish well. It doesn't matter what you have

believe the lies of the Enemy. Get back up. Do whatever you have to do to make it right. Believe God when He says you are a winner; you are victorious. Repeat the apostle Paul's words: "I am able to do all things through Him who strengthens me" (Philippians 4:13).

God knows that you are going to play hurt. He knows this world is broken. But

> *Haven't I commanded you: be strong and courageous? Do not be afraid or discouraged, for the LORD your God is with you wherever you go.*
>
> Joshua 1:9

He also knows that you can finish strong. Scripture is filled with the promises of God that you can receive. For example, 1 John 1:9 promises: "If we confess our sins, He is faithful and righteous to forgive us our sins and to cleanse us from all unrighteousness." That is why God gave us the Scriptures to study, the church to which we can belong, and the faith to believe Him at His Word.

Playing Hurt Means Confessing Your Sin

King David knew what it was like to play hurt. The sins of his life caught up with him so many times, they almost brought him to personal ruin. After his affair with Bathsheba, their son died. Later David's eldest son, Amnon, took advantage of his half-sister (Absalom's sister). This cost Amnon his life.

Absalom, the most rebellious son of the king, waited two years to get revenge—murdering his half-brother, revolting against the kingdom, and declaring himself king. Through all of this, David refused to disengage from God. He never gave up. He stayed in the game.

Read the words of a dying king on his deathbed. No doubt there is a tinge of regret in this statement, but David was sure to give his son and new king, Solomon, the best advice he could. Teaching to the end, David said:

> 2 *"As for me, I am going the way of all of the earth. Be strong and courageous like a man,* 3 *and keep your obligation to the LORD your God to walk in His ways and to keep His statutes, commands, ordinances, and decrees. This is written in the law of Moses, so that you will have success in everything you do and wherever you turn,* 4 *and so that the LORD will carry out His promise that He made to me: 'If your sons are careful to walk faithfully before Me with their whole mind and heart, you will never fail to have a man on the throne of Israel'"* (1 Kings 2:2-4).

Find Out for Yourself

Check out the following Web site for additional help with sin and addiction: **www.settingcaptivesfree.com.**

Also, Google "**Internet pornography filter**" and consider getting one to protect yourself and your family from this modern assault by the Enemy.

Scripture records that even with all the faults and failures, David cried out to God, "Protect me as the pupil of Your eye; hide me in the shadow of Your wings" (Psalm 17:8). Once he was confronted with his own sin, David did not hide it. He was open and honest before the prophet and the Lord:

> "David responded to Nathan, 'I have sinned against the LORD.' Then Nathan replied to David, 'The LORD has taken away your sin; you will not die'" (2 Samuel 12:13).

This kind of open attitude is why Scripture records God saying about David, "I have found David the son of Jesse, a man loyal to me, who will carry out all My will" (Acts 13:22).

You Cannot Change The Past, Only The Future

You can finish strong because your life matters to God. He is far more interested in your future than your past. It takes guts to forget the things of the past and press on toward the future, but you absolutely have to move forward—even though the pain of past sins and mistakes may rise up every day. This is just part of the game; we get knocked down sometimes. God does not want you to give up, give in, or give out. He wants you to finish strong.

The apostle Paul opens up in such an honest way:

> [12] "Not that I have already reached the goal or am already fully mature, but I make every effort to take hold of it because I also have been taken hold of by Christ Jesus. [13] Brothers, I do not consider myself to have taken hold of it. But one thing I do: Forgetting what is behind and reaching forward to what is ahead, [14] I pursue as my goal the prize promised by God's heavenly call in Christ Jesus" (Philippians 3:12-14).

It Is Essential To Engage Your Faith

Paul knew what it meant to play hurt. But he also knew and experienced God in such an intimate way that it did

Coach's Key Point

We were made for God. Ultimate satisfaction and fulfillment in life will come only by living for Him and according to His playbook, the Bible.

Jesus on the Big Screen

AMAZING GRACE

Watch the movie *Amazing Grace* (2006) with your family or friends. After it's over, be sure to discuss the character of John Newton—the former slave-master turned preacher. The most popular hymn ever sung by the church was born out of his experience.

> *Now without faith it is impossible to please God, for the one who draws near to Him must believe that He exists and rewards those who seek Him.*
>
> Hebrews 11:6

not matter what others said, what the Enemy said, or what his circumstances were. Paul truly believed God at His Word. In Hebrews 11:6, the Bible says it is impossible to please God without faith. So live out your faith until the very end. Do not give up. Refuse to quit!

For the Christian, there will be nothing more satisfying than one day being able to say, "God, I gave it my everything. I laid it all out on the field, and I've got nothing left." You already know that you have won the game because you know how the story ends. You already know that one day the sting of death will be gone, and the pain of playing hurt will be erased. The only thing that will reverberate in your ears that day are those all-satisfying words from our Head Coach, "I know you gave it your all, that you played your heart out. Well done, my good and faithful servant. Let's go celebrate!" ✪

1. Jaime Aron, "Chasing Sweetness: Emmit Smith attempts to break Walter Payton's rushing record," *Moscow-Pullman Daily News, Weekend Edition* [online], 26 Oct. 2002 [cited 12 Apr. 2010]. Available from the Internet: news.google.com/newspapers.

VIDEO REVIEW

Watch extra footage of Joe's interview with Ravi Zacharias at **www.LifeWay.com/GamePlan**

SEE SESSION 6 VIDEO LINK ON THE WEB SITE.

GO DEEP

RECOMMENDED RESOURCES FOR DEEPER EXPLORATION ABOUT SIN AND ADDICTION

>> *The Screwtape Letters* by C. S. Lewis

>> *The Purity Principle* by Randy Alcorn

>> *Every Man's Battle: Winning the War on Sexual Temptation One Victory at a Time* by Stephen Arterburn, Fred Stoeker, and Mike Yorkey

DAILY WORKOUTS

MONDAY

Read Psalm 101 and take note of all of the personal commitments from David. Who is he trying to avoid? Who does he want by his side?

¹ *"I will sing of faithful love and justice; I will sing praise to You, LORD.* ² *I will pay attention to the way of integrity. When will You come to me? I will live with a heart of integrity in my house"* (Psalm 101:1-2).

You need to allow people to come into your life to shape who you are. Do you have those people in mind? If not, pray that God will help you find a band of brothers with whom you can do life together.

NOTES

....

....

....

....

For more team info and resources visit // **www.LifeWay.com/GamePlan**

TUESDAY

In *Game Plan for Life*, Ravi Zacharias describes the process for understanding the story of human depravity. When we reject God's rules, we alienate ourselves from God and others. Once this happens, we are dominated by sin and live with guilt.

Can you see this pattern in your own life? In what specific areas have you rejected God's Word and rules for your life? Are you willing to move forward and get help?

[1] *"Therefore, no condemnation now exists for those in Christ Jesus,* [2] *because the Spirit's law of life in Christ Jesus has set you free from the law of sin and of death"* (Romans 8:1-2).

Today, ask God to reveal the truth about who you really are—declared righteous by God when you accept Christ as your Lord and Savior.

NOTES

WEDNESDAY

Read Mark 2:1-12 and notice the teamwork between the men in the story. Use this story as an analogy for understanding the value of teamwork. View yourself as the sick man on the mat, and ask yourself this question: Who do I want and need around me to bring healing in my life?

Pray and ask God to begin developing those relationships that are open and honest. Express the need for accountability and spiritual community to those around you. If you already have those men in your life, thank God for them.

NOTES

THURSDAY

Ravi states, "It has been said that we've attempted to build civilizations when we don't even know what it means to be civilized" (*Game Plan for Life*). Read Romans 1:16-32. Verse 20 says, "Since the creation of the world His invisible attributes, that is, His eternal power and divine nature, have been clearly seen, being understood through what He has made. As a result, people are without excuse."

Are there any lingering excuses that you are hanging on to that enable you to explain away your addiction or habitual sin? If so, make the decision today to stop making excuses. Take responsibility for your actions, confess them to God, and ask Him to guide you as you get help.

NOTES

FRIDAY

The Bible says, "Iron sharpens iron, and one man sharpens another" (Proverbs 27:17). Allow the men in your life to help forge you into the man God wants you be. Don't resist the God-sized wisdom that comes from the wise men in your life.

NOTES

Check out Joe's video devotions at // ***www.LifeWay.com/GamePlan***

Game Plan for Life
by Joe Gibbs with Jerry B. Jenkins

Joe Gibbs's *Game Plan for Life* is a guide to what the Bible says about eleven topics written to "average Joe's" special interests based upon his survey of over 700 men. Edited by best-selling author Jerry Jenkins and in the style of a winning coach, Joe secured contributions from Randy Alcorn, Ravi Zacharias, John Lennox, Tony Evans, Chuck Colson, Josh McDowell, Don Meredith, Walt Larimore, Ron Blue, Ken Boa, and Os Guiness.

   Game Plan for Life inspires readers to live a balanced, God-centered, purpose-filled life, using examples of Coach Gibbs's own storied championship careers as a backdrop to each section. A perfect blend of sports and basic theology, *Game Plan for Life* is designed to bring God's Word home to sports fans (and others) of all generations.

Hero
by Derwin L. Gray

Hero, Unleashing God's Power in a Man's Heart, by Derwin Gray, motivates men to live heroic lives by getting to know the Great Hero so well that His greatness rubs off on them. Men will learn to live with an energized passion, embracing the life they were created to live and leaving a legacy that impacts generations for years to come. Men who long to live the life of a hero or help others live with maximum impact—and women who want to encourage them—will find this book an invaluable guide for the journey.

Group Directory

NAME: _____

ADDRESS: _____

CITY: _____ ZIP CODE: _____

HOME PHONE: _____

MOBILE PHONE: _____

E-MAIL: _____

NAME: _____

ADDRESS: _____

CITY: _____ ZIP CODE: _____

HOME PHONE: _____

MOBILE PHONE: _____

E-MAIL: _____

NAME: _____

ADDRESS: _____

CITY: _____ ZIP CODE: _____

HOME PHONE: _____

MOBILE PHONE: _____

E-MAIL: _____

NAME: _____

ADDRESS: _____

CITY: _____ ZIP CODE: _____

HOME PHONE: _____

MOBILE PHONE: _____

E-MAIL: _____

NAME: _____

ADDRESS: _____

CITY: _____ ZIP CODE: _____

HOME PHONE: _____

MOBILE PHONE: _____

E-MAIL: _____

NAME: _____

ADDRESS: _____

CITY: _____ ZIP CODE: _____

HOME PHONE: _____

MOBILE PHONE: _____

E-MAIL: _____

NAME: _____

ADDRESS: _____

CITY: _____ ZIP CODE: _____

HOME PHONE: _____

MOBILE PHONE: _____

E-MAIL: _____

NAME: _____

ADDRESS: _____

CITY: _____ ZIP CODE: _____

HOME PHONE: _____

MOBILE PHONE: _____

E-MAIL: _____

NAME: _____

ADDRESS: _____

CITY: _____ ZIP CODE: _____

HOME PHONE: _____

MOBILE PHONE: _____

E-MAIL: _____

NAME: _____

ADDRESS: _____

CITY: _____ ZIP CODE: _____

HOME PHONE: _____

MOBILE PHONE: _____

E-MAIL: _____

NAME: _____

ADDRESS: _____

CITY: _____ ZIP CODE: _____

HOME PHONE: _____

MOBILE PHONE: _____

E-MAIL: _____

NAME: _____

ADDRESS: _____

CITY: _____ ZIP CODE: _____

HOME PHONE: _____

MOBILE PHONE: _____

E-MAIL: _____

NAME: _____

ADDRESS: _____

CITY: _____ ZIP CODE: _____

HOME PHONE: _____

MOBILE PHONE: _____

E-MAIL: _____

NAME: _____

ADDRESS: _____

CITY: _____ ZIP CODE: _____

HOME PHONE: _____

MOBILE PHONE: _____

E-MAIL: _____

Leader Overview

This Leader Overview is included in the member book as well as on the CD-ROM for your convenience in leading the Team Training (group session).

TEAM CAPTAIN ICON
When you see the gear in the member book, refer to your Play Sheet for something specific to say or do.

PLAY ICON
When you see this icon, you'll know to start the DVD during Team Training.

TIME
Each session is designed to last 60-90 minutes, depending on your group's schedule and particular dynamic. If you only meet for an hour, try to keep your discussion time limited to the lower amount suggested for each part so you don't run out of time at the end. Try to honor your men's time!

PLAY SHEET
Play Sheets are designed to be cut out of the member book (or printed from the CD-ROM) and attached to a clipboard for use during Team Training. Doing this will allow you to coach with ease and focus on your team. There is information for the group on the Play Sheets that isn't in the member books, so be sure to review the Play Sheet a few days prior to your Team Training.

PREP FOR NEXT WEEK
A checklist is provided at the end of each Play Sheet to remind you of things to review or items to bring to the next session.

CONTACT
Contact your team during the week to encourage them!

RESOURCES & TOOLS
www.LifeWay.com/GamePlan/Leader has additional materials that may be updated to help you maximize the *Game Plan for Life* experience. There are also additional leader resources on the CD-ROM included with the Leader Kit. These include: bulletin insert, poster, promo/invite videos, promo text, media slides, and Web site banners.

Team Captain: Play Sheet 1

Session 01: *You Are Being Scouted*

60-90 minutes

PREGAME 5-10 MINUTES

Open with prayer. Ask God to bless your group's time together and to reveal His will for your lives.

Starting next week, you will use the Pregame to discuss and recap the session from the previous week. But since this is the first week, coach Joe Gibbs will share his heart about the purpose of this study. Before you watch the video, lead the men in your group through the Pregame question below. Let everyone have a chance to briefly share with the rest of the group. **Set the tone for this entire experience by reminding them of this**: "maximum participation makes for a good group experience." This is a team effort.

What are your goals for this six-week study? Write them down in the space provided.

KICKOFF 5-10 MINUTES

Play Video: "Session 01 - You Are Being Scouted"

Lead your team to answer the Kickoff question in the member book. If you have a favorite teacher or coach who made an impact on you, please **share your story first**. After the men share, **highlight** that it was the relational aspect of these coaches or teachers that impacted their lives.

FIRST HALF 15-20 MINUTES

Resume Video: "Session 01 - You Are Being Scouted"
Encourage men to take notes in the space provided in their member books.

HALFTIME 5-10 MINUTES

Lead your men and ask for feedback from the video portion of the first half. **Use the questions** in the member section and be sure to ask if there was anything else that **impacted them** during the video. If you need to take a break, do it now before the second half starts.

SECOND HALF 30 MINUTES

Huddle your group back up for some Bible study. Lead them through the various Scriptures, thoughts, and questions. To keep everyone engaged, have different men read the different passages of Scripture.

Introduce the story of Gideon using the football draft as an analogy. **Say something like,** "The NFL draft happens once a year, and coaches across the nation line up what they think will be their best draft picks. The most sought-after players always go first. They are called "first-round" draft picks. We are going to study someone in Scripture who we would consider an unlikely first-round draft pick, but whom God saw as someone worth having on His team."

2-MINUTE WARNING 5-10 MINUTES

Take this time to **recap the main takeaways** from this lesson.

Challenge your group to reflect on this lesson and go deeper in the Personal Training section throughout the week by reading the articles and doing the Daily Workouts.

PRAYER REQUESTS

Conclude your time by taking prayer requests and praying together as a group.

PREP FOR NEXT WEEK

Be sure to do the following before next week's group:
- ☐ Bring enough Bibles for team members to each have one. You will need them for a demonstration during the 2-Minute Warning.
- ☐ Review next week's Team Training and Play Sheet.
- ☐ Review next week's Kickoff and First Half videos.
- ☐ Contact each team member for encouragement!
- ☐ Have a plan for refreshments.
- ☐ Bring pens, pencils, and paper.

Team Captain: Play Sheet 2
Session 02: *The Ultimate Playbook*
60-90 minutes

PREGAME 5-10 MINUTES

Open with prayer. Ask God to bless your group's time together and to reveal His will for your lives.

Briefly discuss last week's Personal Training. Lead your group through the recap questions found below. If you have a larger group, ask the men to pair up and briefly answer the Pregame questions below. Even though it has only been a week or so, the men in your group may be looking at God in a fresh way. Others may not have experienced anything different. Either way, be sure to encourage them to engage God daily through moments of prayer, Scripture reading, and meditation.

How did your personal training go for the first week? Did anything stand out to you?

Has there been any change in your relationship with God since Session 1? If so, briefly explain.

KICKOFF 5-10 MINUTES

Play Video: "Session 02 - The Ultimate Playbook"

Lead your team to answer the Kickoff questions in the member book. Even though this surface plate metaphor is only briefly explained, it will set up the lesson about God's Word nicely. This illustration communicates two things: (1) the importance of living a balanced life, and (2) that God's Word is the surface plate that lets us know when we are off balance. God's Word is firm and reliable. The idea here is to get the men to think about their attitude toward God's Word—whether or not they respect it, read it, listen to it, and believe it to be true. If you can think of an experience from your past that pertains to this question, **be ready to share** (just in case you need to get the discussion going).

When you are ready to move to the next segment in the video, **say something like**, "Hebrews 4:12 states, 'For the word of God is living and effective' and it judges 'the ideas and thoughts of the heart.' It reveals much about who we are on the inside, and why we do what we do."

FIRST HALF 15-20 MINUTES

Resume Video: "Session 02 - The Ultimate Playbook"
Encourage men to take notes in the space provided in their member books.

HALFTIME 5-10 MINUTES

Lead your men and ask for feedback from the video portion of the first half. **Use the questions** in the member section and be sure to ask if there was anything else that **impacted them** during the video. If you need to take a break, do it now before the second half starts.

SECOND HALF 30 MINUTES

Huddle your group back up for some Bible study. Lead them through the Scriptures and questions while facilitating their discussion. Try to keep everyone engaged. Make sure no one person dominates the discussion. Help everyone who wants to share in the discussion to get a chance to do so.

To **introduce** this story about King Jehoiakim, **say something like**, "Imagine that you are a highly sought-after free agent and have been offered a chance to play for two different teams. The first is the team you currently play for so you are very familiar with them and their playbook. Following that playbook has not brought about the career you would have liked up to this point. The head coach of the other team is so confident in his team's playbook that he invites you to study it and hopes that you will see how you could prosper on his team. As you consider your own abilities and the way you are designed, it seems that you would be a perfect fit on this new team. It's as if the head coach had you in mind when he wrote the playbook."

After question 8, you might **suggest** the Topical Memory System (TMS) by the Navigators or any other Scripture memorization tool that you have found to be successful in your own life.

2-MINUTE WARNING 5-10 MINUTES

Take this time to **recap the main takeaways** from this lesson.

Ask the men to hold a Bible in their hands at the end of this time. **Say something like**, "Men, this is the Word of God. This is the Playbook from our Head Coach. Reflect on that for a few minutes. Feel this book. Turn the pages. Do you believe what you are holding is truly from God? This week, consider what an honor it is for us to have this Playbook that will lead us to victory in life!"

Challenge your group to reflect on this lesson and go deeper in the Personal Training section by reading the articles and dong the Daily Workouts throughout the week.

PRAYER REQUESTS

Conclude your time by taking prayer requests and praying together as a group.

PREP FOR NEXT WEEK

Be sure to do the following before next week's group:
- [ ] Bring a trophy, baseball glove, or football.
- [ ] Review next week's Team Training and Play Sheet.
- [ ] Review next week's Kickoff and First Half videos.
- [ ] Contact each team member for encouragement!
- [ ] Have a plan for refreshments.
- [ ] Bring pens, pencils, and paper.

Team Captain: Play Sheet 3

Session 03: *Making God's Team*
60-90 minutes

PREGAME 5-10 MINUTES

Open with prayer. Ask God to bless your group's time together and to reveal His will for your lives.

Briefly discuss last week's Personal Training. Once you have prayed, lead your group through the recap questions below. If you have a larger group, ask the men to pair up and briefly answer the Pregame questions below. Be sure to **ask** about anything important that came up in the previous meeting, such as if someone asked for prayer about a specific issue, or if there was a need for accountability. As their Team Captain, the important thing is to communicate that you are listening and paying attention to the happenings in their lives.

How did your personal training go for the first week? Did anything stand out to you?

Are you spending more time in God's Word since you worked through Session 2? Explain.

KICKOFF 5-10 MINUTES

Play Video: "Session 03 - Making God's Team"

When you lead your team to answer the Kickoff question, say something like, "the Apostle Paul once said: 'When I was a child, I spoke like a child, I thought like a child, I reasoned like a child. When I became a man, I put aside childish things'" (1 Corinthians 13:11). The idea here is to get the men to think about the difference between the "carefree" attitudes of being a child, and the more "courageous" attitude needed to walk through life as an adult. This distinction will be made clear at the end the Bible study.

Also, if you have something from your past—like a trophy, an old baseball glove, or an old football—that can facilitate telling a good story from your own childhood, **have it ready to share with the group.**

FIRST HALF 15-20 MINUTES

Resume Video: "Session 03 - Making God's Team"
Encourage the men to take notes in the space provided in their member books.

HALFTIME 5-10 MINUTES

Lead your men and ask for feedback from the video portion of the first half. **Use the questions** in the member section and be sure to ask if there was anything else that **impacted them** during the video. If you need to take a break, do it now before the second half starts.

SECOND HALF 30 MINUTES

Huddle your group back up for some Bible study. Lead them through the various Scriptures, thoughts, and questions. To keep everyone engaged, have different men read the different passages of Scripture.

Introduce these two stories using the concept of the "free agent" in professional sports as an analogy. **Say something like,** "It is one thing to be sought after and pursued as a professional athlete, especially if someone is a free agent at the top of their game. But it is another thing for the athlete to commit and sign the contract. We are going to study two different people in Scripture who were personally recruited by Jesus to play on God's team. There were many similarities in these two stories, but what was different was their response."

You may consider leading those who wish to make a decision for Christ in a prayer of trust and faith (see below) or offer them a more private option to hang out after the group meeting. Know your team!

> "Dear Lord Jesus, I know that I am a sinner, and I ask for Your forgiveness. I believe You died for my sins and rose from the dead. I invite You to come into my heart and life. I want to trust and follow You as my Lord and Savior. In Your Name, Amen."

Be sure to rejoice with those who make this decision and guide them in the next steps in following Christ. Here are a few helpful resources to point them toward or perhaps have on hand to give them:
- *Welcome to God's Family* tract by LifeWay Press
- *Survival Kit for New Christians* by Ralph W. Neighbour Jr. and Bill Latham
- *Taking the Next Step* by Ralph Hodge

2-MINUTE WARNING 5-10 MINUTES

Take this time to **recap the main takeaways** from this lesson.

Challenge your group to reflect on this lesson and go deeper in the Personal Training section by reading the articles and dong the Daily Workouts throughout the week.

PRAYER REQUESTS

Conclude your time by taking prayer requests and praying together as a group.

PREP FOR NEXT WEEK

Be sure to do the following before next week's group:
- ☐ Review next week's Team Training and Play Sheet.
- ☐ Review next week's Kickoff and First Half videos.
- ☐ Contact each team member for encouragement!
- ☐ Have a plan for refreshments.
- ☐ Bring pens, pencils, and paper.

Team Captain: Play Sheet 4
Session 04: *The Enemy's Game Plan*
60-90 minutes

PREGAME 5-10 MINUTES

Open with prayer. Ask God to bless your group's time together and to reveal His will for your lives.

Briefly discuss last week's Personal Training. Lead your group through the recap questions found below. If you have a larger group, ask the men to pair up and briefly answer the Pregame questions below. Last week was on the topic of salvation and Making God's Team. Ask if there are any follow-up questions or comments about the lesson.

How did your personal training go for the first week? Did anything stand out to you?

Did you make any life-changing decisions last week that you'd like to share with the group?

Was there anyone on your mind last week with whom you were able to share the gospel?

KICKOFF 5-10 MINUTES

Play Video: "Session 04 - The Enemy's Game Plan"

Lead your team to answer the Kickoff questions in the member book. There are some really good examples already in the world of professional sports concerning athletes who were disqualified for various reasons: Ben Johnson in track and field and Mike Tyson in boxing are just two notorious examples. If you have an example, **be ready to share** in case the men in your group can't think of any.

FIRST HALF 15-20 MINUTES

Resume Video: "Session 04 - The Enemy's Game Plan"
Encourage the men to take notes in the space provided in their member books.

HALFTIME 5-10 MINUTES

Lead your men and ask for feedback from the video portion of the first half. **Use the questions** in the member section and be sure to ask if there was anything else that **impacted them** during the video. If you need to take a break, do it now before the second half starts.

SECOND HALF 30 MINUTES

Huddle your group back up for some Bible study. Lead them through the Scriptures and questions. Try to get everyone involved in the discussion. To keep everyone engaged, have different men read the different passages of Scripture.

To **introduce** this topic, **ask a question like**, "Have you ever known anyone who lied to you about something, and then later tried to lie about the first time they lied? This is the kind of Enemy we are dealing with in life. In the beginning, Satan lied to Adam and Eve about God's Word. Today, he is lying about there ever being an Adam, an Eve, or even a beginning! We'll start this lesson about the Enemy in Genesis because that's where he began his campaign of deception. Genesis 1 and 2 recount the creation of God—which was all good according to the Bible. Immediately following the creation, the Enemy began scheming, attacking, and implementing his game plan. This is key in understanding how badly Satan desires that God be erased from our quest to understand the beginning. If Satan can cast doubt on the story of creation in the first few chapters of God's Word, then he has dismantled the very foundation of the entire Scriptures."

2-MINUTE WARNING 5-10 MINUTES

Take this time to **recap the main takeaways** from this lesson.

Challenge your group to reflect on this lesson and go deeper in the Personal Training section by reading the articles and dong the Daily Workouts throughout the week.

PRAYER REQUESTS

Conclude your time by taking prayer requests and praying together as a group.

PREP FOR NEXT WEEK

Be sure to do the following before next week's group:
- ☐ Review next week's Team Training and Play Sheet.
- ☐ Review next week's Kickoff and First Half videos.
- ☐ Contact each team member for encouragement!
- ☐ Have a plan for refreshments.
- ☐ Bring pens, pencils, and paper.

Team Captain: Play Sheet 5

Session 05: *Signing Bonus*
60-90 minutes

PREGAME 5-10 MINUTES

Open with prayer. Ask God to bless your group's time together and to reveal His will for your lives.

Briefly discuss last week's Personal Training. Lead your group through the recap questions found below. If you have a larger group, ask the men to pair up and briefly answer the Pregame questions below.

Follow up with anything pertinent from the previous week—questions, prayer requests, etc. Take this time to shepherd your group. Give them an encouraging word, and **thank them** for their commitment and attendance. When you pray, ask God to truly bless them.

Were you able to easily recognize the Enemy (and his lies and schemes) last week?

Did you and God win against the Enemy in any sort of way last week? Share it with the group.

KICKOFF 5-10 MINUTES

Play Video: "Session 05 - Signing Bonus"

Lead your team to answer the Kickoff questions in the member book. Depending upon where you are in life, you may be experiencing different challenges. But the idea in the beginning of this lesson is to communicate that the road of personal finances is one we will be racing our entire lives. Use the analogy of the seven-post shaker from the Kickoff to briefly discuss the importance of knowing and understanding the terrain that you are on in life. **Say,** "Preparing for a race should not include impulsive decisions. Rather, you need to get all the information, wisdom, and direction you can so you can be victorious."

FIRST HALF 15-20 MINUTES

Resume Video: "Session 05 - Signing Bonus"
Encourage the men to take notes in the space provided in their member books.

HALFTIME 5-10 MINUTES

Lead your men and ask for feedback from the video portion of the first half. **Use the questions** in the member section and be sure to ask if there was anything else that **impacted them** during the video. If you need to take a break, do it now before the second half starts.

SECOND HALF 30 MINUTES

Huddle your group back up for some Bible study. Lead them through the various Scriptures, thoughts, and questions. Keep everyone engaged, and try not to let just one person dominate the conversation.

Introduce this story about Jesus and money using the signing bonus as an analogy. **Say something like**, "When a star athlete signs on the dotted line to play for a certain team, the salary always seems to hit the headlines. Does anyone know who the highest paid NFL football player is? No matter who it is, and no matter how much he gets paid to play, the point is that he gets to play! But, as we all know, players can be easily distracted by the money and everything that comes with it–fame, riches, houses, etc.

"It is the same when playing on God's team. We can be distracted very easily by the money we make (or don't make). Money is something God lets us use while we're on earth, but as we will see in today's lesson, we need to be conscious and intentional about how we use it. This is one track where we do not want to experience a crash!"

2-MINUTE WARNING 5-10 MINUTES

Take this time to **recap the main takeaways** from this lesson.

Challenge your group to reflect on this lesson and go deeper in the Personal Training section by reading the articles and dong the Daily Workouts throughout the week.

PRAYER REQUESTS

Conclude your time by taking prayer requests and praying together as a group.

PREP FOR NEXT WEEK

Be sure to do the following before next week's group:
- ☐ Review next week's Team Training and Play Sheet. Be sure to review and prepare for the 2-Minute Warning time. Also, check out the Post Game section of the Leader Notes PDF on your CD-ROM.
- ☐ Review next week's Kickoff and First Half videos.
- ☐ Contact each team member for encouragement!
- ☐ Have a plan for refreshments.
- ☐ Bring pens, pencils, and paper.

Team Captain: Play Sheet 6
Session 06: *Playing Hurt*
60-90 minutes

PREGAME 5-10 MINUTES

Open with prayer. Ask God to bless your group's time together and to reveal His will for your lives.

Briefly discuss last week's Personal Training. Lead your group through the Pregame questions below. If you have a larger group, ask the men to pair up and briefly answer the pregame questions. Since this is the last follow-up time scheduled for *Game Plan for Life: Group Edition*, the second question pertains to the entire group experience. **Ask** the men to share an encouraging word if they have broken through and experienced victory in any area of their lives—no matter how great or small. **Applaud them**, literally, and celebrate any and all victories over the Enemy.

How did the daily workouts challenge you to make some changes and adjustments with your finances?

Are there any victories from last week (or the previous weeks) that you would like to share?

KICKOFF 5-10 MINUTES

Play Video: "Session 06 - Playing Hurt"

Lead your team to answer the Kickoff questions in the member book. God created all of us to experience community on some level in our lives. The team concept is not a new concept, and that is why we are taking this approach when talking about sin and addiction. It is a dangerous thing for a wounded man to be left to himself.

These questions are designed to get your group of men thinking about the value of being on a team. Hopefully, the men in your group will have experienced "team" life at some time in their past. But if they haven't experienced it, hopefully this lesson will inspire them to pursue community, accountability, and teamwork.

FIRST HALF 15-20 MINUTES

Resume Video: "Session 06 - Playing Hurt"
Encourage the men to take notes in the space provided in their member books.

HALFTIME 5-10 MINUTES

Lead your men and ask for feedback from the video portion of the first half. **Use the questions** in the member section and be sure to ask if there was anything else that **impacted them** during the video. If you need to take a break, do it now before the second half starts.

SECOND HALF 30 MINUTES

Huddle your group back up for some Bible study. Lead them through the various Scriptures, thoughts, and questions. Before you get started, thank them for being here and for finishing strong. Let them know you appreciate their commitment.

To **introduce** this lesson, **say something like**, "Men, it is God's desire for us that we live a life without succumbing to habitual sin or addiction of any kind. God's expectation is found in 1 John 3:9. To paraphrase, it basically says that everyone on God's team does not keep on sinning as if they were on the other team. God changes who you are in Christ, and you have the power to defeat sin. God also expects us to live differently because He understands the very nature of addiction, and He wants to protect us from that horrible, defeated experience. 2 Peter 2:19 says, 'They promise them freedom, but they themselves are slaves of corruption, since people are enslaved to whatever defeats them.'

"In this game called life, the number-one treatment for a man who is playing hurt is to develop authentic friendships with other God-centered men and to live life in the context of that spiritual community. It is a dangerous thing for a wounded man to be left to himself—on the field without support and encouragement. Let us take a look at the power of teamwork on God's team, and how that helps us overcome the challenges we face when we are playing hurt."

2-MINUTE WARNING 5-10 MINUTES

Take this time to **recap the main takeaways** from this lesson.

Challenge your group to reflect on this lesson and go deeper in their relationship with God by focusing on ways they can be active players on God's team from here on out.

▶ **Play Video: "Joe's Closing Challenge"**

Ask your men to write down the top two or three things they have received from completing this study. Ask your group if they have a desire to keep meeting. If so, **talk about it** right now. If your group needs to take a break for a period of time before meeting again, **schedule it** right now. If there are several men who want to group up into smaller accountability groups, then **encourage them** to look at their calendars right now. **DON'T PUT OFF THE PLANNING!** The point is to walk away from this last meeting with a plan already in place for your men. Additional study materials are suggested at the Web site www.LifeWay.com/GamePlan/Leader as well as on the CD-ROM.

PRAYER REQUESTS

Conclude your time by taking prayer requests and praying together as a group.